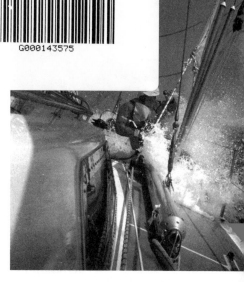

Emmett Dulaney

MCSE

FAST TRACK

Windows NT Workstation 4

New Riders

201 West 103rd Street, Indianapolis, Indiana 46290

MCSE FAST TRACK:
WINDOWS NT WORKSTATION 4

International Standard Book Number: 1-56205-938-6

Library of Congress Catalog Card Number: 98-86319

Printed in the United States of America

First Printing: September, 1998

00   99   98   4   3   2   1

TRADEMARKS

WARNING AND DISCLAIMER

Executive Editor
Mary Foote

Acquisitions Editor
Steve Weiss

Development Editor
Nancy Warner

Managing Editor
Sarah Kearns

Project Editor
Christopher Morris

Copy Editor
Cheri Clark

Indexer
Becky Hornyak

Technical Editors
Andrew Brice
Grant Jones

Book Designers
Nathan Clements
Ruth Lewis

Cover Designer
Sandra Schroeder

Production
Cheryl Lynch
Megan Wade

Contents at a Glance

TABLE OF CONTENTS

ABOUT THE AUTHOR

Emmett Dulaney, MCP+I, MCSE is a consultant for D S Technical Solutions and an instructor for a national training company. He has been teaching certification courses for the continuing education department of Indiana University/Purdue University at Fort Wayne for over four years and is the Certification Corner columnist for *NT Systems Magazine*. In addition, Emmett is the author or co-author of more than a dozen computer books, including *CNE Short Course, Teach Yourself MCSE Windows NT Workstation in 14 Days,* and *MCSE TestPrep: TCP/IP*. He has also written more than 100 magazine articles on computing for several publications.

ABOUT THE TECHNICAL REVIEWERS

R. Andrew Brice currently works as a senior instructor for ProSoft I-Net Solutions in Austin, Texas. His certifications include Novell CNA and CNE, as well as the Microsoft Certified Trainer and Microsoft Certified Systems Engineer in both Windows NT 3.51 and 4.0. Since 1991, he has been providing consulting in network design and support to small and large organizations, including Fortune 1000 companies. This consulting has included training for Novell, Microsoft, and Netscape technical curricula, coupled with web-site development, security, and e-commerce. He specializes in the design and implementation of wide area networks (WANs). He credits his accomplishments to the love and support provided by both his wife, Susan, and his daughter, Katie. He can be reached via the Internet at andrewb@flash.net.

Grant Jones has worked as a network engineer for the past five years, and is certified as an MCSE, MCP + Inet, MCT, CNE3/4 (Certified NetWare Engineer versions 3 and 4), and CNI (Certified NetWare Instructor). For the past three years, Grant has been teaching the official Microsoft core classes along with IIS and TCP/IP; he is currently working for ProSoft I-Net Solutions, where he is creating courseware for ePC certifications. Grant has written courses on Netscape Mail and IIS 4.0; the course he developed on IIS 4.0 was taught to Microsoft Visual Basic programmers in Redmond, WA. In addition, Grant has spoken at trade shows such as Internet World and Internet Commerce Expo on Internet fundamentals and electronic commerce.

DEDICATION

For Karen.

ACKNOWLEDGMENTS

First and foremost, I would like to thank Steve Weiss for his conviction and belief in the product and for his patience with it, as well. I would also like to thank Nancy Warner, Andrew Brice, Grant Jones, and Christopher Morris.

TELL US WHAT YOU THINK!

As the reader of this book, *you* are our most important critic and commentator. We value your opinion and want to know what we're doing right, what we could do better, what areas you'd like to see us publish in, and any other words of wisdom you're willing to pass our way.

As the Executive Editor for the Certification team at Macmillan Computer Publishing, I welcome your comments. You can fax, email, or write me directly to let me know what you did or didn't like about this book—as well as what we can do to make our books stronger.

Please note that I cannot help you with technical problems related to the topic of this book, and that due to the high volume of mail I receive, I might not be able to reply to every message.

When you write, please be sure to include this book's title and author, as well as your name and phone or fax number. I will carefully review your comments and share them with the author and editors who worked on the book.

Fax: 317-581-4663

Email: certification@mcp.com

Mail: Mary Foote
         Executive Editor
         Certification
         Macmillan Computer Publishing
         201 West 103rd Street
         Inidanapolis, Indiana 46290

Introduction

The *MCSE Fast Track* series is written as a study aid for people preparing for Microsoft Certification exams. The series is intended to help reinforce and clarify information the student is already familiar with. This series is not intended to be a single source for student preparation, but rather a review of information and set of practice materials to help increase the likelihood of success when the student takes the actual exam.

WHY WE DID THIS SERIES: WORDS FROM THE AUTHOR AND PUBLISHER

First, let us state this once more: New Riders' *MCSE Fast Tracks* are not intended to be single sources for exam preparation. These books have been uniquely written and developed to work as supplements to your existing knowledge base.

But exactly what makes them different?

1. **Brevity.** Many other exam training materials seek Microsoft approval (you've probably seen the official "Microsoft Approved Study Guide" logo on other books, for example), meaning they must include 50% tutorial material and cover every objective for every exam in exactly the same manner and to the same degree. MCSE Fast Tracks *break away from that mold by focusing on what you really need to know to pass the exams.*

2. **Focus.** *Fast Tracks* are targeted primarily to those who know the technology but who don't yet have the certification. No superfluous information is included. *MCSE Fast Tracks* feature only what the more-experienced candidate needs to know to pass the exams. Fast Tracks *are affordable study materials for the experienced professional.*

3. **Concentrated value and learning power.** Frankly, we wouldn't be surprised if *Fast Tracks* prove to appeal to a wider audience than just advanced-level candidates. We've tried to pack as much distilled exam knowledge as possible into *Fast Tracks*, creating a "digest" of exam-critical information. No matter what level you're at, you may see this digest on certification training as a logical starting point for your exam study.

4. **Classroom-tested, instructor-proven.** With tens of thousands of new certification candidates entering the training routine each year, trainers like Emmett Dulaney—on the forefront of the certification education lines—are finding themselves in front of classes comprised of increased numbers of candidates with the following:

- already a measurable base of understanding of the technology

- a desire for efficient "just-the-facts" training

Emmett and New Riders pooled their thoughts and found that no books *truly* existed that adequately fill this need:

To provide an easy way to review the key elements of each certification technology without being bogged down with elementary-level information and to present this information in the light of an insider's perspective.

Emmett developed his instructional style and content to help this ever-increasing group of nonbeginners, and they in turn helped him focus the material even more. He then worked with New Riders to develop this classroom-tested material into a refined, efficient self-instruction tool. What you see in this book is the result of that interaction.

Think of *Fast Tracks* as the set of instructor's notes you always wished you could get your hands on. These notes only truly help you if you already know the material and are ready to take on the exam itself. It's then that this book is truly designed to help you shine. Good luck and may your hard work pay off.

WHO SHOULD READ THIS BOOK

The Windows NT Workstation book in the *MCSE Fast Track* series is specifically intended to help students prepare for Microsoft's Implementing and Supporting Microsoft Windows NT Workstation 4.0 (70-073) exam—one of the client electives available in the MCSE program.

PART I: WHAT THE WORKSTATION EXAM (70-073) COVERS

The Implementing and Supporting Microsoft Windows NT Workstation 4.0 certification exam measures your ability to implement, administer, and troubleshoot Windows NT Workstation 4.0 computer systems. It focuses on determining your skill in seven major categories:

- Planning
- Installation and Configuration
- Managing Resources
- Connectivity
- Running Applications
- Monitoring and Optimization
- Troubleshooting

The Implementing and Supporting Microsoft Windows NT Workstation 4.0 certification exam uses these categories to measure your ability. Before taking this exam, you should be proficient in the job skills covered in the following pages.

Planning

The Planning section of the exam is designed to make sure that you understand the hardware requirements of Windows NT Workstation 4.0. The knowledge needed here also requires an understanding of general networking concepts.

Objectives for Planning

- Create unattended installation files.

- Plan strategies for sharing and securing resources.

- Choose the appropriate file systems to use in a given situation. File systems and situations include the following:

  - NTFS

  - FAT

  - HPFS

  - Security

  - Dual-boot systems

Installation and Configuration

The Installation and Configuration part of the Workstation exam tests you on virtually every component of the product.

Objectives for Installation and Configuration

- Install Windows NT Workstation on an Intel platform in a given situation.

- Set up a dual-boot system in a given situation.

- Remove Windows NT Workstation in a given situation.

- Install, configure, and remove hardware components for a given situation. Hardware components include the following:

  - Network adapter drivers

  - SCSI device drivers

  - Tape device drivers

  - UPSs

  - Multimedia devices

  - Display drivers

- Keyboard drivers

- Mouse drivers

♦ Use Control Panel applications to configure a Windows NT Workstation computer in a given situation.

♦ Upgrade to Windows NT Workstation 4.0 in a given situation.

♦ Configure server-based installation for wide-scale deployment in a given situation.

Managing Resources

The Managing Resources component concentrates on daily administration issues.

Objectives for Managing Resources

♦ Create and manage local user accounts and local group accounts to meet given requirements.

♦ Set up and modify user profiles.

♦ Set up shared folders and permissions.

♦ Set permissions on NTFS partitions, folders, and files.

♦ Install and configure printers in a given environment.

Connectivity

The Connectivity component of the Workstation certification exam concentrates on how to use the various interconnecting components of the TCP/IP protocol and others.

Objectives for Connectivity

♦ Add and configure the network components of Windows NT Workstation.

♦ Use various methods to access network resources.

- Implement Windows NT Workstation as a client in a NetWare environment.
- Use various configurations to install Windows NT Workstation as a TCP/IP client.
- Configure and install Dial-Up Networking in a given situation.
- Configure Microsoft Peer Web Services in a given situation.

Running Applications

The Running Applications component of the Implementing and Supporting Microsoft Windows NT Workstation 4.0 exam has only two objectives.

Objectives for Running Applications

- Start applications on Intel and RISC platforms in various operating system environments.
- Start applications at various priorities.

Monitoring and Optimization

The Monitoring and Optimization component of the NT Workstation 4.0 certification exam focuses on performance issues.

Objectives for Monitoring and Optimization

- Monitor system performance by using various tools.
- Identify and resolve a given performance problem.
- Optimize system performance in various areas.

Troubleshooting

The Troubleshooting component of the certification exam has seven components running the entire gamut of troubleshooting.

Objectives for Troubleshooting

◆ Choose the appropriate course of action to take when the boot process fails.

◆ Choose the appropriate course of action to take when a print job fails.

◆ Choose the appropriate course of action to take when the installation process fails.

◆ Choose the appropriate course of action to take when an application fails.

◆ Choose the appropriate course of action to take when a user cannot access a resource.

◆ Modify the Registry using the appropriate tool in a given situation.

◆ Implement advanced techniques to resolve various problems.

HARDWARE AND SOFTWARE RECOMMENDED FOR PREPARATION

The *Fast Track* series is meant to help you review concepts with which you already have training and hands-on experience. To make the most of the review, you need to have as much background and experience as possible. The best way to do this is to combine studying with working on real networks using the products you will be tested on. This section describes the minimum computer requirements you will need in order to build a solid practice environment.

Computers

The minimum computer requirements to ensure that you can study on everything you'll be tested on include one or more workstations running Windows 95 or NT Workstation and two or more servers running Windows NT Server, all of which are connected by a network.

Workstations: Windows 95 and Windows NT

- Computer on the Microsoft Hardware Compatibility List

- 486DX 33MHz

- 16MB of RAM

- 200MB hard disk

- 31/2-inch 1.44MB floppy drive

- VGA video adapter

- VGA monitor

- Mouse or equivalent pointing device

- Two-speed CD-ROM drive

- Network Interface Card (NIC)

- Presence on an existing network or use of a hub to create a test network

- Microsoft Windows 95 or NT Workstation 4.0

Servers: Windows NT Server

- Two computers on the Microsoft Hardware Compatibility List

- 486DX2 66MHz

- 32MB of RAM

- 340MB hard disk

- 3 1/2-inch 1.44MB floppy drive

- VGA video adapter

- VGA monitor

+ Mouse or equivalent pointing device

+ Two-speed CD-ROM drive

+ Network Interface Card (NIC)

+ Presence on an existing network or use of a hub to create a test network

+ Microsoft Windows NT Server 4.0

OBJECTIVE REVIEW NOTES

The Objective Review Notes feature of the *Fast Track* series contains a separate section—two to a page—for each subobjective covered in the book. Each subobjective section falls under the main exam objective category, just as you'd expect to find it. It is strongly suggested that you review each subobjective and immediately make note of your knowledge level; then return to the Objective Review Notes section repeatedly and document your progress. Your ultimate goal should be to be able to review only this section and know if you are ready for the exam.

Suggested use:

1. Read the objective. Refer to the part of the book where it's covered. Then ask yourself the following questions:

   + Do you already know this material? Then check "Got it" and make a note of the date.

   + Do you need some brushing up on the objective area? Check "Review it" and make a note of the date. While you're at it, write down the page numbers you just checked, because you'll need to return to that section.

   + Is this material something you're largely unfamiliar with? Check the "Help!" box and write down the date. Now you can get to work.

2. You get the idea. Keep working through the material in this book and in the other study material you probably have. The more you get the material, the quicker you can update and upgrade each objective notes section from "Help!" to "Review it" to "Got it."

3. Cross reference the materials YOU are using. Most people who take certification exams use more than one resource at a time. Write down the page numbers of where this material is covered in other books you're using, or which software program and file this material is covered on, or which video tape (and counter number) it's on, or whatever you need that works for you.

Think of this as your personal study diary—your documentation of how you beat this exam.

PART II: ROUNDING OUT YOUR EXAM PREPARATION

Part II of this book is designed to round out your exam preparation by providing you with the following chapters:

- "Fast Facts Review" is a digest of all "What Is Important to Know" sections from all Part I chapters. Use this chapter to review just before you take the exam: It's all here, in an easily reviewable format.

- "Insider's Spin on Exam 70-073" grounds you in the particulars for preparing mentally for this examination and for Microsoft testing in general.

- "Sample Test Questions" provides a full-length practice exam that tests you on the actual material covered in Part I. If you mastered the material there, you should be able to pass with flying colors here.

- "Hotlist of Exam-Critical Concepts" is your resource for cross-checking your tech terms. Although you're probably up to speed on most of this material already, double-check yourself anytime you run across an item you're not 100 percent certain about; it could make a difference at exam time.

- "Did You Know?" is the last-day-of-class bonus chapter: A brief touching-upon of peripheral information that's designed to be helpful and of interest to anyone using this technology to the point that he or she wishes to be certified in its mastery.

What's Important to Know About Exam 70-073

MCSE Fast Track: Windows NT Workstation 4 is written as a study aid for people preparing for Microsoft Certification Exam 70-073. The book is intended to help reinforce and clarify information with which the student is already familiar. This series is not intended to be a single source for exam preparation, but rather a review of information and set of practice tests to help increase the likelihood of success when taking the actual exam.

Part I of this book is designed to help you make the most of your study time by presenting concise summaries of information that you need to understand to succeed on the exam. Each chapter covers a specific exam objective area as outlined by Microsoft:

1   **Planning**

2   **Installation and Configuration**

3   **Managing Resources**

4   **Connectivity**

5   **Running Applications**

6   **Monitoring and Optimization**

7   **Troubleshooting**

ABOUT THE EXAM

Exam Number	**70-073**
Minutes	**90***
Questions	**51***
Passing Score	**705***
Single-Answer Questions	Yes
Multiple-Answer with Correct Number Given	**Yes**
Multiple-Answer Without Correct Number Given	No
Ranking Order	**No**
Choices of A–D	Yes
Choices of A–E	**No**
Objective Categories	**7**

*Note: These exam criteria will no longer apply when this exam goes to an adaptive format.

▶ Create unattended installation files.

▶ Plan strategies for sharing and securing resources.

▶ Choose the appropriate file system to use in a given situation. File systems and situations include these:
   • NTFS
   • FAT
   • HPFS

▶ Security

▶ Dual-boot systems

CHAPTER 1

Planning

COMPARING OPERATING SYSTEMS

Currently, Microsoft is actively promoting three operating systems: Windows 95/98, Windows NT Workstation 4.0, and Windows NT Server 4.0.

At A Glance: Hardware Requirements

Minimum Requirements	Windows 95/98	Windows NT Workstation 4.0	Windows NT Server 4.0
Processor	386DX/20	486DX/33	486DX/33
RAM	4MB	12MB	16MB
Free space	40MB	120MB	130MB

Windows 95/98 is designed to work with various peripherals and legacy systems and provide ease of use. It offers Plug and Play features, supports preemptive multitasking, is available only for the Intel platform, and can network in a workgroup or domain-based network. Windows 95/98 cannot be a server (performing centralized authentication and security) or make use of multiple processors.

Windows NT Workstation 4.0 is an operating-system product almost identical to the server, but tweaked for client use. It offers the same networking features as Windows 95/98 but does not utilize Plug and Play. It can be run on Intel or RISC-based machines (including MIPS, Alpha, and PowerPC), and it utilizes multiprocessing and multitasking. It is designed for compatibility with DOS 5.0+, OS/2 2.x, Windows 3.x, and POSIX applications. It differs most significantly from Windows 95/98 in the area of security: To use files or printers, a user must be authenticated.

Windows NT Server 4.0 differs from Workstation in that it offers services for Macintosh clients, RAID fault tolerance, domain login validation, directory replication, 256 possible remote access sessions (as opposed to 1 with Workstation), and an unlimited number of concurrent connections (as opposed to 10 with Workstation). It also can handle more processors, includes Internet Information Server (Workstation has Peer Web Services), and offers advanced services such as DNS, DHCP, and WINS.

Further differences are that Server is the only product that can act as a domain controller, and that Workstation preloads a Virtual DOS

Machine (VDM) at startup to speed the first load of an older application (Server does not do this to conserve memory). Additionally, Server cannot participate in a workgroup unless it is configured as a standalone server.

DRIVE CONFIGURATIONS

Partitions are logical organizations of a physical disk. A disk can be subdivided into several partitions—each formatted separately. Windows NT assigns a different drive letter to each partition, and the user is free to interact with each as if it were a completely separate disk.

There are two types of partitions: primary and extended. There can be up to four primary partitions, and these are the only ones that can be booted. If you elect to use an extended partition (of which only one can be used per disk), the maximum number of primary partitions drops to three. The extended partition can be subdivided into as many as four logical drives, though none of them is bootable.

If you install Windows NT into an active partition, the partition remains active. If you install it into another partition, that partition then becomes active. The two main partitions under Windows NT are the system and boot partitions, as depicted on a normal system.

At A Glance: Crucial Windows NT Drives

Drive	Contents	Partition
C:	Boot files	System partition
D:	Windows NT system files	Boot partition

The counterintuitive naming of the partitions can be confusing; you must always remember that the boot partition contains the system files, and the system partition contains the boot files.

CREATING PARTITIONS

Before NT is installed, FDISK is the tool to use for creating partitions in most Microsoft operating systems. If NT has been installed, Disk Administrator is the Windows NT tool for anything and everything related to disks.

To use Disk Administrator to create primary partitions, follow these steps:

1. Select an area of free space on a disk.
2. Choose Partition | Create. A box indicating possible minimum and maximum sizes for a new primary partition appears.
3. In the Create Primary Partition dialog box, enter the size of the partition you want to create, and click OK.

Creating an extended partition with Disk Administrator is done very similarly:

1. Select an area of free space on a disk.
2. Choose Partition | Create Extended. A box indicating possible minimum and maximum sizes for a new primary partition appears.
3. In the Create Extended dialog box, enter the size of the extended partition you want to create, and click OK.

You create a logical drive within an extended partition by selecting the extended partition and choosing Partition | Create.

CREATING UNATTENDED INSTALLATION FILES

The first file needed for an unattended installation is the UNATTEND.TXT file, which, along with the uniqueness data file, controls how Workstation is set up. Having the same format as an INI file, it can be used *only* to configure Windows NT Workstation and cannot be used directly to configure other applications.

NOTE   As a point of clarification, although the UNATTEND.TXT file does not directly install applications, it can be used to call and initiate the installation of applications.

The UNATTEND.TXT File

To instruct Windows NT setup (WINNT.EXE or WINNT32.EXT) to use an unattended installation file, you must put a /U: on the command line followed by the full path and filename of the unattended installation file, such as this:

```
WINNT /U:A:\SPENCER.TXT /B
```

This command line will use the unattended installation file in drive A called SPENCER.TXT and copy the boot files to the drive so that no floppy swapping will be needed. All files used with the unattended installation must fit within the 8.3 character limitation of DOS.

A sample UNATTEND.TXT file is included with the Windows NT 4.0 Resource Kit on the CD-ROM, as shown here:

```
; Microsoft Windows NT Workstation Version 4.0 and
; Windows NT Server Version 4.0
;(c)1994 - 1996 Microsoft Corporation. All rights reserved.
;
; Sample Unattended Setup Answer File
;
; This file contains information about how to automate the installation
; or upgrade of Windows NT Workstation and Windows NT Server so the
; Setup program runs without requiring user input.
;
; For information on how to use this file, read the appropriate sections
; of the Windows NT 4.0 Resource Kit.

[Unattended]
OemPreinstall = no
ConfirmHardware = no
NtUpgrade = no
Win31Upgrade = no
TargetPath = WINNT
OverwriteOemFilesOnUpgrade = no

[UserData]
FullName = "Your User Name"
OrgName = "Your Organization Name"
ComputerName = COMPUTER_NAME

[GuiUnattended]
TimeZone = "(GMT-08:00) Pacific Time (US & Canada); Tijuana"

[Display]
ConfigureAtLogon = 0
BitsPerPel = 16
XResolution = 640
YResolution = 480
VRefresh = 70
AutoConfirm = 1
```

```
[Network]
Attend = yes
DetectAdapters = ""
InstallProtocols = ProtocolsSection
JoinDomain = Domain_To_Join

[ProtocolsSection]
TC = TCParameters

[TCParameters]
DHCP = yes
```

This file makes a good starting point from which to customize for your own installations. The section headings are enclosed in brackets, and there are several key sections worth noting, as discussed in the following subsections.

[UNATTENDED]

The [Unattended] section of the unattended installation file must be present or the file will be ignored. It determines what, if any, of the rest of the file will be processed during setup. These are some key entries:

♦ OEMPreinstall must be yes or no, with the default being no. A no value means that the OEM directory will not be copied or used.

The sections entitled [MassStorageDrivers], [KeyboardDrivers], [PointingDeviceDrivers], [OEMBootFiles], and [OEM_Ads] must all be present if the OEMPreinstall is set to yes.

♦ NoWaitAfterTextMode is used to prevent Windows NT from prompting for a key before rebooting after the text mode portion of setup. The value of 1 tells NT not to wait after text mode for a keystroke.

♦ NoWaitAfterGuiMode is similar to NoWaitAfterTextMode but is used to prevent Windows NT from prompting for a keystroke at the end of the GUI mode setup.

♦ ConfirmHardware specifies whether the user should confirm hardware (no is the default and should be used for unattended installation).

- NTUpgrade indicates how the setup program should handle existing installations of NT. Generally this option should be set to no to prevent the script from accidentally overwriting an existing version of NT.

- TargetPath specifies where NT will be installed. If the option is *, the setup program will generate a unique directory name.

[UserData]

The [UserData] section is used to set up the username, company name, and computer name. Under a normal installation, the FullName and OrgName are the only values supplied.

[Network]

This section is important to getting a fully functional unattended installation file because most Windows NT workstations, especially those that would need an unattended installation file, are installed on a network. These are the key options:

- Attended specifies whether NT should prompt the installer for information on the network—defeating most of the reasons for using an unattended installation file.

- JoinWorkgroup is mutually exclusive with the JoinDomain option and specifies the workgroup that the workstation should join.

- JoinDomain specifies the domain that the workstation should be installed in.

- CreateComputerAccount allows the unattended installation to automatically create a computer account in the domain for the computer being installed.

The Uniqueness Database File (UDF)

Most of the entries that exist in an unattended installation file can be overwritten by a uniqueness database. The uniqueness database is simply a standard text file that—like the unattended installation file—uses INI file type sections and entries.

The command-line switch to use a UDF file is /UDF:*ID*,[*FileName*]. The *ID* can be alphanumeric and must match an ID in the uniqueness database. If missing, the assumed filename is $UNIQUE$.UDB, and it is also assumed to be on a floppy disk that the user will be prompted for.

The first section of a UDF file is [UniqueIds], which tells the setup program which IDs are contained in the file and which sections each of those IDs uses. A sample follows:

```
[UniqueIds]
SPENCER=UserData, GuiUnattended, Network
KRISTIN=UserData, GuiUnattended, Network
EVAN=UserData, GuiUnattend, Network
```

After you've established the [UniqueIds] section of a UDF file, you need to set up the sections themselves. These sections are identical to the unattended installation file. You create the same headings and entries, understanding that some entries can't be in the UDF file. Here's an example:

```
[SPENCER:UserData]
FullName = "HP 133 Pentium"
OrgName = "D S Tech"
ComputerName = SPENCER

[KRISTIN:UserData]
FullName = "HP 166 MMX Pentium"
OrgName = "STEEN REALTY"
ComputerName = KRISTIN

[EVAN:UserData]
FullName = "HP 233 Pentium Pro"
OrgName = "D S Tech"
ComputerName = EVAN
```

Entries in this file will override the entries in the unattended installation file if they are present. If the entries are not present in the installation file, the values from the UDF will be used as if they were in the unattended installation file.

The OEM Directory

Unattended installations can install more than just the base Windows NT installation, and most of the functionality for adding additional applications is handled via the OEM directory stored under the distribution directory.

This directory can be located almost anywhere. It allows custom HALs, drivers, and other files to be used in the setup, as well as for system files to be replaced, entire directory structures to be created, and programs to be run. In the root of the OEM directory is a file called CMDLINES.TXT that contains the commands you want to execute after the completion of the GUI portion of the setup.

Most often, the OEM directory structure is used to run the SYSDIFF program—the recommended tool for building an unattended installation.

One of the design limitations of having setup copy files from the text mode of the setup routine is that long filenames are not necessarily supported. Because of this, all the files in the OEM directory must have short filenames that fit the 8.3 naming standard of DOS. This doesn't, however, preclude the use of programs that use or need long filenames. Each directory under the OEM directory can contain a file called $$RENAME.TXT. This file controls how setup will rename files from their 8.3 names to long filenames.

The file is very simple, and it also follows the INI file format. The file can contain multiple sections, which indicate the directories that the files are in. By default, the $$RENAME.TXT file works on files in the current directory. A sample follows:

```
[]
KAREN.LNK="Karen Employee File.lnk"
DONNA.LNK="Donna Master Copy of Employee Manual.lnk"
EMPLOY.LNK="Corporate Employee Menu.lnk"
```

The short filename is listed first, followed by an equal sign, followed by the long filename in quotation marks. Even though the file format is simple, it's important to type the filenames correctly. A single error can prevent the installation from occurring as it was intended.

SYSDIFF

SYSDIFF is an automated tool designed to allow you to quickly and easily replicate most environments. Like any automated tool, SYSDIFF has its limits. One of the limits is that the installation directory must be in the same place on both the system creating the difference file and the machine that the difference file is applied to. This means that if you generate a difference file from a machine with Windows NT installed in the `c:\WINNT` directory, every other machine on which you utilize the difference file must have Windows NT installed in `c:\WINNT` as well.

The SYSDIFF tool has five modes:

- `/snap`: Create a snapshot
- `/diff`: Create a differences file
- `/apply`: Apply a differences file
- `/dump`: Display the contents of a differences file
- `/inf`: Create the `$OEM$` structure

SYSDIFF works by creating a snapshot of the system before applications are installed or configuration settings are changed with the `/snap` mode. After the snapshot has been created, the updates are made to the system and then the `/diff` mode is used to create a differences file. The differences file can be moved from machine to machine and is designed to allow programs to be added to the system in an automated fashion.

After the differences file has been copied to another system, it can be applied using the `/apply` mode. This will make the same changes to the new computer that were recorded between when the snapshot was created and when the differences file was created on the original system. The `/dump` and `/inf` modes are used to debug and tweak the differences file.

SHARING AND SECURING RESOURCES

Windows NT Workstation 4.0 can function as a standalone operating system or in one of two types of networks:

- Workgroup
- Domain

A workgroup is a number of computers networked together for the purpose of sharing resources among themselves. There is no server, and the resources are shared on the peer machines.

With a domain, there is at least one server—a machine dedicated to authenticating users and governing the resources they are allowed to share. With a domain, you have "user" level security, meaning that all resource access is based on the users who authenticated themselves during the logon. With Windows NT Workstation, you still have user authentication taking place, the main difference being distributed versus centralized.

These are the key differences between the models:

- In a workgroup, each workstation that shares resources must have a user account for the user trying to use the resource, or the guest account must be enabled.

- In a domain, there are many ways to assign permissions to resources. Microsoft recommends that access to resources be assigned to local groups and then the local groups added to global groups in the domain.

The Workstation test, unlike the Server and Enterprise tests, has only a limited number of questions about domains, and you need to know that Workstation works in both environments. How to implement it within those environments is discussed in Chapters 3, "Managing Resources," and 4, "Connectivity."

Do know, however, the networking protocols that can be used in either environment. Those protocols are summarized in the following section.

CHOOSING A PROTOCOL

Protocols are standards or languages that computers use to talk with each other in a network. Microsoft Windows NT 4 (both Server and Workstation) differs from previous versions of Windows NT in that it installs TCP/IP as the default protocol. The other two available protocols are the same as those that existed in previous versions of NT.

At A Glance: Networking Protocols

Protocol	Installed	Main Benefits	Main Drawback
TCP/IP	By default	Routable, language of the Internet, industry standard	Management
NWLink	By administrator	Routable, needed for compatibility with NetWare	Used only for NetWare compatibility
NetBEUI	By administrator	Small overhead, fast, used for compatibility with older Microsoft networks	Non-routable, uses broadcasts for address resolution

NOTE

During most installations, both TCP/IP and NWLink are selected.

TCP/IP is the protocol originally used with the UNIX hosts. UNIX hosts were almost exclusively the hosts comprised by the Internet until a few years ago. With the growth in popularity of the Internet and the need to communicate using a common protocol, TCP/IP has quickly become the de facto standard used for networking today. It benefits greatly from being available for all platforms and easily routed. Its only real requirement is that each host must have a unique IP address. TCP/IP supports DHCP, DNS, and WINS, all of which are discussed in the next section.

NWLink is a protocol compatible with IPX/SPX—the networking protocol used by NetWare servers. It is needed on the Windows NT Server if you must service NetWare clients or interact with NetWare servers or if you are attempting to migrate from NetWare to NT. NWLink is also easily routed (as is IPX/SPX).

NetBEUI is the protocol originally used in Microsoft's Windows for Workgroups and LAN Manager networking products. Ideal for department-sized LANs, it cannot be routed (although it can be used with a bridge), and it is primarily used now only for compatibility with existing networks.

CHOOSING AN APPROPRIATE FILE SYSTEM

Windows NT Workstation is capable of running on two types of *file systems*: FAT and NTFS. Technically, it can install into three types: FAT, NTFS, and unformatted. When discussing FAT, however, it is important to know that the inference is to VFAT, though that is no longer specifically spelled out. The original FAT accompanied DOS, and it is available in versions through 6.22. VFAT became available with the initial release of Windows 95. FAT32 became available with Windows 95 Release B (an OEM-only release). FAT32 is currently available only in Windows 95B and Windows 98, and it is incompatible with Windows NT Server.

At A Glance: File System Features

Feature	FAT	VFAT	FAT32	NTFS
Filename length	8.3	255	255	255
8.3 compatibility		Yes	Yes	Yes
Maximum files in root directory	512	512	No limit	No limit
Maximum files in nonroot directory	65,535	No limit	No limit	No limit
Partition size	2GB	4GB	4TB	16EB
Local security	No	No	No	Yes
Transaction tracking	No	No	No	Yes
Hot fixing	No	No	No	Yes
Overhead	1MB			>2MB (avg. 4.5–10)
Required for dual booting	Yes	Yes	No	No
Required for RISC-based	Yes	Yes	No	No
Accessible from DOS	Yes	Yes	Yes	No

continues

At A Glance: continued

Feature	FAT	VFAT	FAT32	NTFS
Accessible from OS/2	Yes	Yes	No	No
Case sensitive	No	No	No	POSIX only
Case preserving	No	Yes	Yes	Yes
Compression on file level	No	No	No	Yes
Efficiency	<200MB	200–400MB	<400MB	>400MB
Convertible	To NTFS only	To NTFS only	No	No
Fragmentation level	High	High	High	Low
Extensible attributes	No	No	No	Yes

An important note is that HPFS—OS/2's High Performance File System—is no longer supported as of Windows NT 4.0; it was supported in Windows NT prior to this release.

The CONVERT.EXE utility can be used at any time to convert a FAT partition into an NTFS partition without losing any data. There is no such utility for converting from NTFS to FAT, and to do so you must back up the data, reformat the hard drive, and restore the backup.

WHAT IS IMPORTANT TO KNOW

The following bullets summarize the chapter and accentuate the key concepts to memorize for the exam:

- The minimum Intel-based hardware requirements for Windows NT Workstation 4.0 are a 486DX/33 processor with 12MB of RAM and non-ESDI disks.

- The command-line option for using an unattended installation script is /U:*filename*.

- The command-line option for using a uniqueness database file is /UDF:*ID,filename*.

- Not all options in the unattended installation file can be specified in the uniqueness database file; however, a single uniqueness database file can contain multiple IDs, so a single uniqueness database file can contain unique settings for multiple systems.

- The OEM structure allows complete control of the installation process, but files in the OEM structure must conform to the 8.3 DOS file-naming convention.

- $$RENAME.TXT file controls the renaming of files in the OEM directory.

- SYSDIFF must be run with the /snap mode to create a snapshot first. After the applications are installed and the configuration is changed, the /diff mode is used to create a differences file from the snapshot that can be applied to multiple computers (via the /apply mode).

- SYSDIFF can create a completely different OEM directory from a differences file by using the /inf option.

▶ Install Windows NT Workstation on an Intel platform in a given situation.

▶ Set up a dual-boot system in a given situation.

▶ Remove Windows NT Workstation in a given situation.

▶ Install, configure, and remove hardware components for a given situation. Hardware components include the following items:
  • Network adapter drivers
  • SCSI device drivers
  • Tape device drivers
  • UPSs
  • Multimedia devices
  • Display drivers
  • Keyboard drivers
  • Mouse drivers

▶ Use Control Panel applications to configure a Windows NT Workstation in a given situation.

▶ Upgrade to Windows NT Workstation 4.0 in a given situation.

▶ Configure server-based installation for wide-scale deployment in a given situation.

CHAPTER *2*

Installation and Configuration

INSTALLING ON THE INTEL PLATFORM

Before installing Windows NT Workstation 4.0, you should verify that your hardware is compatible. Beneath the SUPPORT directory of the operating system CD-ROM is an HCL.HLP (Hardware Compatibility List Help file), which will show you what hardware was capable of running Windows NT when the product was first released. Updated versions of this file are available on the Web at

www.microsoft.com/hwtest/hcl/

Additionally, in the \SUPPORT\HQTOOL directory of the CD-ROM, there is a batch file called MAKEDISK.BAT. This batch file allows you to create a hardware qualification disk. Boot your system from that disk, and it will create an NTHQ.TXT file, which will list all the hardware components that Windows NT is detecting in your system. Compare this with the HCL to verify that your system can run Windows NT properly before continuing with the installation.

Windows NT can be installed from one of two files, WINNT.EXE or WINNT32.EXE.

At A Glance: Installation Utilities

File	Purpose	To Install Over
WINNT32.EXE	Upgrade previous versions of Windows NT	Windows NT 3.5x
WINNT.EXE	Install Windows NT from scratch	Everything except Windows NT 3.5x

Unless you are specifically upgrading from a previous version of Windows NT, WINNT.EXE is the installation utility you use. The default directory into which it will attempt to place the operating system is WINNT, but you can change this to any directory you want. If you install into a directory that is already holding an operating system, you are replacing one operating system with another. If you install into a directory that does not currently have an operating system, you are creating a dual-boot machine. *Dual booting* is available with previous or current versions of Windows NT Workstation, Windows NT Server, Windows 95, and DOS. The former two you can dual-boot or upgrade from, whereas the latter two you cannot upgrade from.

You begin normal installation by summoning the Windows NT CD-ROM from within your current operating system, as shown in Figure 2.1.

When you select Windows NT Setup via the button in the upper-right corner, a DOS window is automatically started, WINNT is called, and you're asked to specify which location the installation files will be coming from, as shown in Figure 2.2.

On an Intel machine, the directory will be I386; on an Alpha machine, the directory will be ALPHA; and so on.

By default, WINNT will require you to reboot the machine and boot from a set of three bootable floppies. If you do not have these floppies, you can create them from the CD-ROM with the /OX parameter, or you can choose not to boot from them with the /B parameter. Some WINNT parameters and their purposes are listed here:

WINNT Parameters	Purpose
/B	No boot floppies
/C	Do not check for available free space
/F	Do not verify files as they are copied to the hard disk
/I	Specifies the filename (no path) of the setup information file, with the default being DOSNET.INF
/OX	Make the three bootable floppies
/S	Alternative source file location
/T	Put temporary files in a specified location
/U	Unattended installation (requires a filename)
/UDF	Unattended installation for installing on multiple machines (requires a filename)

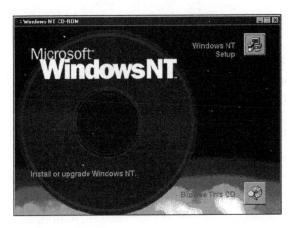

FIGURE 2.1
The opening installation screen from the CD-ROM.

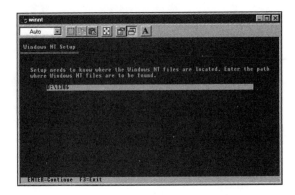

FIGURE 2.2
The file source location must be specified.

There are four phases to the installation process:

1. Pre-Installation—During this phase, necessary files are copied over.

2. Gathering Information—The Setup Wizard queries you about how the workstation should be set up.

3. Installing Windows NT Networking—Network cards, protocols, and so on are located and specified at this point.

4. Finishing Setup—Information specific to the system is given, such as time zone and monitor settings.

Pre-Installation

During Pre-Installation, the files copy to your hard disk. After the copying phase completes, you must reboot your system. It is imperative that you remove any floppies from the drive before finishing.

After the reboot, the Windows NT Workstation Setup screen appears and offers you four key choices:

- Enter: Continues with the installation

- R: Lets you repair a damaged operating system by reinstalling key files but leaving data intact

- F1: Offers Help about the operation

- F3: Exits the installation

For normal installation, press Enter, and the recognized mass storage devices (hard drives and so on) are listed. If some of your drives are not found, you can press S to specify them. You can also press F3 to exit or Enter to continue.

The Microsoft licensing agreement appears. Press Page Down to page down through it, reading it carefully. After you have read and understand all of it, press F8 to continue.

All of your identified hardware, such as keyboard and mouse, are listed. If you do not agree with the list, make the appropriate changes. When you do agree with the list, press Enter to continue.

Partitions on your hard drive are listed. Select the one into which Windows NT Server is to be installed, and press Enter. You can now choose to format your partition selection as FAT, partition it as NTFS, convert it from FAT to NTFS, or leave it as it is. After making your selection, press Enter, specify a target directory location, and press Enter again.

Windows NT Server Setup prompts you to perform an examination of the drive the partition is on. By default, it wants to do an exhaustive search for corruption. You can shorten the search (making it less exhaustive) by pressing Esc. Otherwise, press Enter to continue.

After the search, files are copied to your hard drive into the directory you specified (WINNT, by default). After the copying, remove the floppies and press Enter to reboot. Following the reboot, there are a very few seconds of additional file copying, and then you are finished with the Pre-Installation phase.

Phase 0 is now complete.

Gathering Information

You must choose between one of four setup options:

♦ Typical: The default

♦ Portable: Recommended for laptops

♦ Compact: Does not install any optional components

♦ Custom: Pick and choose what you want

Next, enter your name and organization in the first dialog box that appears. This information is entered into the Registry and is used by default in installation dialog boxes for all new software you install. Click Next when you have entered the values.

Enter the CD-ROM key for your license, and click Next. After doing so, you must specify a computer name of up to 15 characters in length. This name identifies the computer and thus must be unique. This is also the NetBIOS name that can be used for name resolution with WINS (Windows Internet Naming Service).

You must next choose and confirm a password for the Administrator account. Two accounts are created during the installation of Windows NT Workstation 4.0:

♦ The *Guest* account, because it is so limited, does not require you to assign a password during installation.

♦ The *Administrator* account, on the other hand, is very powerful (by virtue of being a member of the Administrators group), and you are prompted for a password. Said password can be nothing (press Enter) or up to 14 characters in length. After the installation is complete, you can change the password at any time as you would for a regular account.

Next, you are prompted to make an *ERD* (Emergency Repair Disk). This is a backup of the Registry for the system. You can make—and are recommended to make—ERDs on a regular basis after installation via the RDISK utility.

Select to install the most common components, or choose which components you want to install (games and so on).

Phase 1 is now complete.

Installing Windows NT Networking

Windows NT Workstation 4.0 can be configured without networking, or for networking through a wire to the network or remotely accessing the network. In most scenarios, *wired to the network* is the likely choice, and this is the default.

The next order of business is to install the adapter by picking it from the list or loading drivers from disk. If you do not have a recognizable adapter installed, you can choose MS Loopback from the list, and the Microsoft Loopback Adapter will act as though there is an adapter in your machine even if there is not.

Select the protocols you want to use (TCP/IP is chosen by default; the other two choices are IPX/SPX-compatible and NetBEUI).

For TCP/IP configuration, you must specify whether you are using a DHCP server to supply the data or manually entering an IP address. The IP address must be unique within the realm of all hosts the server can communicate with.

After this information is configured, networking services are started. You must give a computer name that is unique throughout the company's network. Even if networks are connected over a WAN, it is strongly recommended that all NetBIOS names be unique. You cannot set up an NT machine, or any other MS machine, without having a unique NetBIOS name.

Choose whether the workstation will participate in a workgroup or domain, and specify the appropriate name.

Phase 2 is now complete.

Finishing Setup

As Finishing Setup begins, program groups are created and added to the desktop. You must then select the appropriate time zone and set the display characteristics (you can save no changes until you first test the display at those settings). Following this, the accessory files (Clipboard, Paint, and so on) are copied to their appropriate positions.

The configuration is saved and you are prompted to insert a disk that will be used to create the ERD (only if you opted to create an ERD previously in the installation process). Following such, you must remove all media from the system and restart the computer. The installation is now complete.

Phase 3 is complete.

SETTING UP A DUAL-BOOT SYSTEM

During the initial installation discussion, it was pointed out that if you install Windows NT Workstation into any directory other than where the original operating system was, dual booting is configured by default. This works well as long as NT is the last operating system added to the system. If another operating system is added after NT, however, the new operating system will take control away from NT's Boot Manager, and the dual boot will no longer exist.

To correct this problem complete the following steps:

1. Create a Windows NT Emergency Repair Disk using the RDISK utility.

2. Shut down NT and install the new operating system.

3. Boot with the setup floppy 1.

4. Insert setup floppy 2 when prompted.

5. Select Repair when you reach the initial welcome screen.

6. When asked which things you want setup to do, deselect everything except Inspect boot sector.

7. Specify or allow NT to detect hard disk controllers.

8. Insert your emergency repair disk. Press Enter when prompted.

9. Remove the emergency repair disk, and reboot the computer.

Windows NT has now been restored, and there will be an option on the boot menu for the other operating system you installed.

REMOVING WINDOWS NT

Should you need to remove Windows NT from a computer, first determine whether there are any NTFS partitions on the computer. If there are any NTFS partitions on the computer, you must remove them because Windows 95, 98, and other operating systems cannot use them. If the NTFS partitions contain only data and no Windows NT system files, you can use the Windows NT Disk Administrator program to remove them. If the NTFS partitions contain Windows NT system files, or if they are logical drive(s) in an extended partition, you cannot use the MS-DOS FDISK utility to remove them.

After you have removed all the NTFS partitions, you need to start the computer with a Windows 95 or MS-DOS system disk that contains the SYS.COM file. Then type the command sys c: to transfer the Windows 95 or MS-DOS systems files to the boot track on drive C. You then need to remove all the remaining Windows NT Workstation files, as listed here:

- All paging files (C:\Pagefile.sys)

- C:\BOOT.INI, C:\BOOTSECT.DOS, C:\NTDETECT.COM, C:\NTLDR (these are hidden, system, read-only files)

- The winnt_root folder

- The c:\Program files\Windows Windows NT folder

> **WARNING**
>
> If you fail to remove the Windows NT boot track from your computer, the following error message appears when you restart your computer:
>
> BOOT: Couldn't find NTLDR.
> Please insert another disk.
>
> You can fix this by running SYS C: from a Windows 95 or MS-DOS boot disk.

If you are dual booting Windows NT and another operating system (such as MS-DOS or Windows 95), create a startup disk for the other operating system before you uninstall Windows NT. If MS-DOS, Windows 3.x, or Windows 95 doesn't boot properly after you remove NT, boot to the startup disk and type SYS C: to reinstall your basic operating system files onto the hard drive.

> **NOTE**   To create a startup disk in Windows 95, go to the Add/Remove Programs applet in Control Panel and select the Startup Disk tab.

Very much worthy of note is the fact that the SYS.COM file is not copied when a system disk is created. This file must be manually copied to the floppy.

INSTALLING AND CONFIGURING HARDWARE COMPONENTS

Windows NT 4.0 does not have support for Plug and Play, and most hardware components must be configured through Control Panel applets to make the hardware work. Two exceptions to this statement would be PCI-based devices and PCMCIA cards, which do—almost always—automatically configure themselves, even in Windows NT.

The Windows NT exam focuses on determining which applet is used to add or configure hardware. The next several sections cover the hardware that is specifically mentioned in the exam guidelines.

Network Adapter Drivers

One of the most common additions to a Windows NT Workstation is a network card, as more and more systems at home and at work are being networked. A network card is becoming an essential part of every computer, not just those used in large business.

Adding network adapters is handled in the same Network Control Panel applet that all network services are installed in. An Adapters tab in the Network applet is used to configure adapters.

Most of the devices listed have a properties sheet that you can modify. The properties sheet allows you to configure the hardware resources that the card will use and any network card–specific properties such as which interface to use.

To get to the properties of a network adapter, you can either double-click on the adapter in the list or click on the adapter once and then click Properties.

The properties of a network card are also shown when the card is installed. If you click the Add button on the Adapters tab, you get a list of all the network adapters whose drivers ship with Windows NT. If you don't find your adapter on this list, you can press the Have disk button to enter the path where the drivers for your adapter can be found.

SCSI Device Drivers

Even if you don't have a SCSI controller in your system, NT behaves as if you do. As far as Windows NT is concerned, any disk controller not supported by BIOS is a SCSI controller and as such is configured via the SCSI Control Panel applet.

Both the controller and any attached devices have properties sheets that can be accessed via the Properties button. Simply select the device or controller that you want to view settings for and click the Properties button. A properties dialog box will be displayed. Even though you will be able to see the resources via the properties dialog boxes, you will not be able to change them.

To actually change the SCSI device drivers installed in NT, you must select the Drivers tab of the SCSI Adapters dialog box. If you want to add a new SCSI controller to your system, you can do so by clicking the Add button. This will raise a dialog box that prompts you to identify the model of SCSI controller you're installing. When you click OK, your SCSI controller will raise a properties dialog box for any properties that it needs to have configured.

Tape Device Drivers

After you've installed SCSI controllers, you'll need to back up the disks. This is generally done via a tape drive. Tape drives are essential to NT because they are used to back up the system. The backup utility included with Windows NT will back up only to tape; it will not back up to floppy disks or removable media such as Zip or Jaz disks.

All tape devices are controlled through the Tape Devices applet, which has two tabs, Devices and Drivers. The Devices tab is very similar to the SCSI Adapters tab except that it is only a single level because tape devices don't have devices connected to them and because there is a Detect button.

The properties of the tape drive are the same ones that were visible in the SCSI Adapters applet, containing basic information, as well as the SCSI ID and firmware revision of the device.

You can add a new device by clicking the Detect button. At this point, Windows NT will scan through its database of drivers and attempt to load the appropriate ones. Normally, this detection will be successful.

If the detection isn't successful, you can click on the Drivers tab, and click the Add button. This will display a list of tape drives supported by Windows NT. After clicking OK, you'll be prompted for the Windows NT media so that NT can copy files. It will not be necessary to reboot NT for the tape driver to be installed.

UPS

Next to a tape drive, UPS, or Uninterruptible Power Supply, is probably the second most important "safety" device for computers. UPSs allow computers to continue operating even if there is a short interruption in power from the utility company.

UPSs come in various capacities and sizes. The smallest UPSs for PCs are about 250 VA. Large data center UPSs can be well in excess of 100KVA. A VA is a voltage-amp. It refers to the amount of power that a UPS can output. At normal 110 volt output, a 250VA UPS can output about 2 amps of current. This is enough to drive a small PC and a 14-inch monitor, but it wouldn't sustain a high-end PC with a 17-inch monitor.

The other characteristic of UPSs, which isn't normally listed prominently on their specification sheets, is how long these devices can keep your computer running. UPSs are devices that utilize a battery to supply power, and batteries have a finite amount of power that they can supply before giving out.

Because NT likes to be shut down properly in the event of a power loss, it provides a simple UPS monitoring utility that can be used to signal Windows NT when it is time to shut down because the UPS has been activated and the battery is about to fail. This utility causes Windows NT to shut down when the UPS is about to fail, allowing NT to try to get shut down successfully.

Multimedia Devices

Multimedia devices, such as sound cards, video capture cards, and joysticks, are all controlled from the Multimedia applet. When you open the Multimedia applet, the Multimedia Properties dialog box will appear. To add or configure a device, you must select the Devices tab.

Configuring a device is as simple as selecting the device and then clicking the Properties button. You might be confronted with a related Settings button that you must also click to change the settings of the device.

Adding a device is equally simple. Simply click the Add button, and then select your device from the list that appears or insert a disk and select Unlisted or Updated driver. The driver will raise any settings dialog boxes that it needs completed for operation.

Display Drivers

Every Windows NT system has a video card. Windows NT requires at least a VGA-compatible video card in order to work. Windows NT controls this video card through the Display applet.

The Display applet controls not only the specifics of the video card and monitor used with NT but also the background, the screen saver, the color schemes, the desktop, and, if IE 4.0 is installed, the appearance of the Web as well.

To change the video card drivers or monitor refresh rates, click on the Settings tab. The settings on this tab are based on what the video card is capable of doing. Unlike in Windows 95, this dialog box doesn't take into account the limitations of the monitor.

You can change the color depth without worrying about whether the monitor will be able to handle it; however, you need to test both the resolution and the refresh rate before applying the changes. Windows NT will inform you that you need to test the settings if you don't test them before clicking the Apply button.

Keyboard Drivers

The most familiar input device used is the keyboard. With the invention of 104-key keyboards, "natural" key keyboards, and such, it is possible that you'll need to load drivers other than that for the standard 101/102-key keyboard most users use. For the test you will need to know that you can change the keyboard driver via the Keyboard Control Panel applet.

Mouse Drivers

With the advent of Windows, the mouse became the second most important input device. Should you for any reason need to change your mouse, you will need to go to the Mouse Control Panel applet.

USING CONTROL PANEL APPLICATIONS TO CONFIGURE WORKSTATION

The Control Panel was the topic in the preceding discussion, and the same information addressed there is pertinent here. The following table includes the information that you should know about each Control Panel applet to pass the Workstation test:

Applet	Function
Accessibility Options	Controls options for changing the way in which Windows operates to make it easier for those with physical impediments. This is where you would change settings if keys need to be held down, or to ignore some repeated keystrokes, or to be notified with a sound when toggle keys such as Caps Lock are pressed. You can also choose to have Windows show you each time a sound is made, or allow you to use the keyboard as if it were a mouse.
Add/Remove Programs	Enables you to install or remove compatible 32-bit applications and change which Windows NT options have been installed.
Console	Controls how DOS sessions appear within Windows NT.
Date/Time	Enables you to change the time and date; also enables you to change the time zone.
Dial-Up Monitor	Displays connection information and enables current dial-up connections to be terminated.
Fonts	Displays the fonts directory, enabling you to add, delete, and view fonts.
Mail and Fax	Enables you to change the services installed in MAPI profiles and to manage MAPI profiles, which are used in mail-enabled applications such as Microsoft Exchange and Microsoft Outlook.

Applet	Function
Modems	Maintains information on each modem installed and on the geographic location of the system so that Windows NT can make adjustments to telephone numbers dialed to accommodate changing locations.
ODBC	Installs and removes drivers for remote databases and other data sources used by applications such as Access.
Regional Settings	Controls the way in which Windows NT displays numbers, currency, dates, and times.
Services	Lists all the installed services and allows you to start, stop, or pause them. Also allows you to change how the services start up.
System	Controls system-level settings such as hardware and user profiles, environment variables, virtual memory, and startup options.

UPGRADING TO WINDOWS NT WORKSTATION 4.0

Windows NT can upgrade earlier versions of Windows NT and only two other operating systems:

- Windows 3.1
- Windows for Workgroups 3.11

Windows NT will perform an upgrade only if the directory into which Windows NT is installed is the same as the directory that these operating systems were installed in.

Windows NT cannot upgrade Windows 95, OS/2, UNIX, or any other operating system.

When Windows NT upgrades a previous version of Windows NT, virtually all the settings are maintained, including the security database, common and personal groups, file associations, and so forth. Windows NT might not be able to migrate certain settings, such as video card settings, because the video driver structure was changed.

When upgrading Windows 3.1 or Windows for Workgroups 3.11, Windows NT keeps the groups, the file associations, and the Registry.

CONFIGURING SERVER-BASED INSTALLATIONS FOR WIDE-SCALE DEPLOYMENT

If you can remember nothing else for the exam, remember this: Server-based installations work only for Intel-based systems, and RISC-based systems must be installed via a local CD.

That said, the first step in configuring a server-based installation is to copy the \i386 directory from the Windows NT CD-ROM to a shared directory on a Windows NT or Windows 95 shared folder, or to copy it to a location on a NetWare volume. After the files have been copied to the share, next copy the unattended files. You should copy at least the unattended installation file and any files and directories in the OEM directory structure, but you might want to copy the uniqueness database file as well.

After the installation is complete, issue the WINNT or WINNT32 command against the shared directory with the /b option to eliminate the need for the floppy disks and with the /U and /UDF options to specify the unattended file and uniqueness database files, respectively.

WHAT IS IMPORTANT TO KNOW

The following bullets summarize the chapter and accentuate the key concepts to memorize for the exam:

♦ The WINNT program is used to install Windows NT on a machine that is already running DOS, Windows 3.x, or Windows 95.

♦ The WINNT32 program is used to install Windows NT on a machine that is already running a previous version of Windows NT.

♦ The WINNT and WINNT32 option /b copies boot files to the local hard drive so that boot floppies aren't needed. By default, WINNT and WINNT32 create startup floppy disks.

♦ Windows NT can be installed via (1) a floppy with a CD, (2) a bootable CD, or (3) a network.

♦ RISC-based computer can be installed only via a bootable CD.

♦ The NT Hardware Qualifier (NTHQ) can be used to determine whether there are any problems in the hardware that will prevent Windows NT from installing correctly.

♦ All hardware that has passed Windows NT testing is listed in the hardware compatibility list (HCL), available on the Windows NT CD, TechNet, and Microsoft's Web site.

♦ Windows NT can upgrade only Windows 3.1, Windows for Workgroups 3.11, and previous versions of Windows NT. Windows 95 cannot be upgraded to Windows NT.

♦ Creating server-based installations is as easy as copying the \i386 directory to a shared directory on a server. The *server* can be Windows NT, Novell NetWare, or a Windows 95 shared folder. It's not important what server software the server is running.

♦ To create a dual-boot situation with Windows NT when there is already an installed operating system, simply install Windows NT into a separate directory.

♦ Creating a dual-boot situation with Windows NT if there isn't a previously installed operating system requires the use of an emergency repair disk.

♦ Windows NT does not support Plug and Play.

♦ Windows NT does not have an Add New Hardware Control Panel applet.

♦ Network adapters are installed via the Network Control Panel applet.

- The Network Adapters section of the Network Control Panel is a catchall for communications devices, such as multiport boards, that aren't specifically supported somewhere else.

- Windows NT treats all hard disk controllers as if they were SCSI controllers if they are not supported via BIOS.

- Tape drives are installed via the Tape Drives Control Panel applet. For the most part, only SCSI tape drives are supported.

- Uninterruptible Power Supplies (UPSs) and Standby Power Supplies (SPSs) are configured through the UPS Control Panel applet.

- Sound cards, video capture cards, MIDI cards, and other multimedia cards are handled through the Multimedia Control Panel applet.

- Display adapter settings are changed via the Display Control Panel applet. Windows NT allows you to change the resolution, color depth, and refresh frequency. Windows doesn't require a reboot when any of these settings is changed, but the settings must be tested to ensure that they will work with your monitor.

- Changing the color depth doesn't require that the settings be tested because all monitors support all color depths.

- Changing the display driver requires that the system be rebooted. Automatic detection requires that the computer be rebooted twice.

- Keyboard drivers are changed in the Keyboard Control Panel applet.

- Mouse drivers are changed in the Mouse Control Panel applet.

- The Accessibility Options Control Panel applet contains ways of easing access for those with difficulty using the keyboard or hearing computer sounds, as well as controlling the capability to use the keyboard as a mouse.

- The Add/Remove Programs Control Panel applet is used to add, remove, or change installation options for compatible Win32 applications.

- The Regional Settings Control Panel applet is used to change how numbers, times, and dates are displayed.

▶ Create and manage local user accounts and local group accounts to meet given requirements

▶ Set up and modify user profiles

▶ Set up shared folders and permissions

▶ Set permissions on NTFS partitions, folders, and files

▶ Install and configure printers in a given environment

CHAPTER 3

Managing Resources

UNDERSTANDING USER ACCOUNTS

In Windows NT, there are only two ways users get rights and permissions to resources:

- They are explicitly assigned a right or permission through their account.

- They are members of a group that has a right or permission.

Windows NT User accounts, with their unique identifier, allow a user to log on to the Windows NT network, and thus the user's access token (account/password combination) is his access ticket to all resources on the Windows NT network.

Windows NT Workstation user accounts are created in User Manager. To create a new account, the user running User Manager must be a member of either the Administrators or the Power Users group.

User Properties

Each user has several properties pages. When a new user is being created, the first screen, shown in Figure 3.1, allows for individual settings.

This user properties dialog box displays such items as the user's name and password, and how to handle the changing of that password. Specifically, each setting is set as described in the following list.

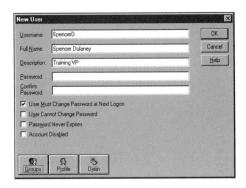

FIGURE 3.1
The New User dialog box and its settings.

- **Username.** This is the name that each user will use to log on to the network. This name must be unique in the domain. The name must be no longer than 20 characters and cannot contain the characters " / \ [ ] : ; | = , + * ? < >. The goal of enterprise networking is for each user in the enterprise to have only *one* user account.

- **Full Name.** This allows for the display of the user's full name. You can use this as a sort setting by selecting View | Sort by Full Name.

- **Description.** This setting is copied from account to account if used as a template. It is used to further describe a user.

- **Password/Confirm Password.** The password for the user can be up to 14 characters long and is case sensitive.

Of the five properties at the top of the dialog box, only the description will be copied from account to account. All other settings must be reentered for a copied user.

The lower settings in the user properties dialog box relate to how passwords will be handled. These are the settings:

- **User Must Change Password at Next Logon.** This approach forces the user to change her password when she next logs on to the network.

- **User Cannot Change Password.** This selection is used in higher-security networks where the users are assigned passwords for their account.

- **Password Never Expires.** This setting overrides the account policy of password expiration and should be used only for service accounts in Windows NT.

- **Account Disabled.** This setting prevents the user from using this account.

Group Properties

The Group properties are used to assign the user whose account you are modifying to various groups. The corresponding dialog box is shown in Figure 3.2.

This dialog box only allows the assignment of users to groups.

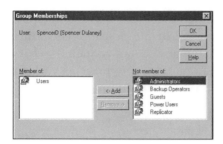

FIGURE 3.2
The Group Memberships dialog box and its settings.

User Environment Profile

The User Environment Profile dialog box, shown in Figure 3.3, is one of the main configuration pages.

The User Environment Profile dialog box allows the administrator to configure the following items as centrally located:

♦ User profile path

♦ Login script

♦ Home directory

The main purpose in centrally locating these options is that you can have all of these items stored on a central server. When users store their profiles and home directories centrally, the process of backing up data is more manageable.

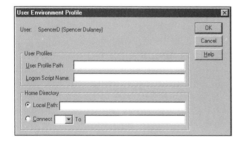

FIGURE 3.3
The User Environment Profile dialog box and its settings.

User Profile Path

The User Profile Path designates a specific location on a specified server where the user's profile will be stored. As the directory structure reveals, the profile path contains the user portion of the Registry in the file NTUSER.DAT. The directory structure itself also contains a user's Start menu, desktop layout, and recently used file listing. By using this profile path, users can have their desktops and personal configuration settings follow them to whichever Windows NT computer they use.

The most common path that is entered for the user profile path is \\SERVER\PROFILESHARE\%USERNAME%. It should be noted that this location is server specific. Consideration should be given to locating the user's profile on a server in the same subnet as the client to limit WAN traffic. Roaming profiles are supported only in domain environments, and directory replication can be used to copy the profiles to multiple servers (see the *Windows NT Server Fast Track* book for more information on this topic).

If you rename the roaming profile from NTUSER.DAT to NTUSER.MAN, it becomes a "mandatory profile." The user can make changes to the environment, but all changes are lost when the user logs off.

Login Script

The login script will allow an administrator to configure common drive mappings, run central batch files, and configure the system. When configuring a login script, simply insert the name of the *.bat or *.cmd file that you want to execute. The logon scripts are stored by default in the directory

```
\%systemroot%\system32\repl\import\scripts
```

This directory could exist on a Windows NT Workstation or, if it is a member of a domain, on the domain controller.

This directory is shared as the netlogon share. The main purpose of the logon script is to present a common network layout to all clients on the network.

Home Directory

The home directory setting for the user's profile will create a personal directory where the user can store data on a network server. The most common entry used for creating home directories is to create a common share called USERS. Assuming that this share has been created, you would enter that path for each home directory as \\COMPUTER\USERS\%USERNAME%.

Dialin Properties

The Dialin Information dialog box, shown in Figure 3.4, allows the administrator to determine which users are granted dial-in access to the network and whether call-back security is to be implemented.

If No Call Back is selected, the user can immediately use network resources. This is commonly used in low-security networks and for users working out of hotel rooms.

If Set By Caller is selected, the user is prompted to enter the phone number where he is located presently, and the Remote Access Server calls him back at that number.

If Preset To is configured, the user dials in to the office network. Upon connection, the line is dropped, and the user is called back at a predefined phone number. This is the setting to use if you are at all concerned about security, because you are verifying that the user is at a specified location.

Template Accounts

As an administrator, you should consider creating template user accounts for the various types of users that you would see yourself creating. This would enable you to quickly create new user accounts when required. These template accounts should be disabled to prevent their use on the network for network access.

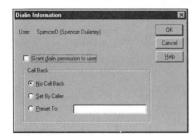

FIGURE 3.4
The Dialin Information dialog box.

To use the template account to your advantage, just select the template account in User Manager and create a copy of the account by selecting User | Copy (or pressing F8). This action copies all properties of the template account except for the following properties:

+ Username

+ Full Name

+ Password

+ Confirm Password

Template accounts also work best when you use the %USERNAME% environment variable for both the user profile path and the home directory. This also enables the option User Must Change Password at Next Logon while disabling the Account Disabled check box.

One last note: It is always preferable to rename an account than to copy an existing account because renaming keeps the same permissions and descriptions as the original. Once deleted, group and user accounts cannot be undeleted. They must be re-created, and then permissions and restrictions must be manually assigned. You can rename accounts very easily, because they are really identified to the system by a Security Identifier (SID).

At the risk of redundancy, to create templates, the system administrator creates an account (just like a standard user account); sets all the groups, hours, dial-in properties, and so forth; and then only has to copy the account and change the fields that differ.

Windows NT Group Accounts

Knowledge and testing on the usage of global and local groups is one of the key differences between the Windows NT Workstation, Core, and Enterprise exams. For Workstation, know that you can create only local groups because the creation of global groups requires Windows NT Server. Know also the basics of the two types of groups and their major differences.

Differences Between Global and Local Groups

One of the most difficult enterprise technologies to get a handle on is the difference between *global* groups and *local* groups. In an Enterprise network, we emphasize the acronym AGLP to define the use of global and local groups.

AGLP stands for Accounts/Global Groups/Local Groups/Permissions. This means that to assign permissions to any resource, you must perform the following steps:

1. Make sure that user accounts exist for each user who will need access to the resource.

2. Assign all user accounts to a common global group. If the users are spread across multiple domains, you will have to create a global group in each domain. This is because global groups can contain only users from the domain in which they are located. Always use a preexisting global group if one exists, and create new global groups only if you have to.

3. Assign the global groups from each domain to a local group in the domain where the resource exists. If the resource is on a Windows NT Domain Controller, it is created on a domain controller. If the resource is on a Windows NT Workstation or Windows NT Member Server, the local group is created on that system's local account database.

4. Assign necessary permissions to the local group.

Local groups are the only groups that should be assigned permissions. When assigning local group permissions, the administrator should always determine whether there is an existing local group with the appropriate permissions. For example, suppose you want to grant a user the ability to create new users or change group memberships. Because the Power Users group already has these permissions, there is no reason to create a new local group to perform this task.

The local groups that are found only on Windows NT workstations or member servers are Power Users. They have almost identical permissions as Administrators with one key difference: They can create accounts, but not ones with Administrator-level permissions.

The local groups found on all Windows NT systems include these:

- Administrators
- Backup Operators
- Guests
- Replicator
- Users

The Administrators group is found on all Windows NT–class computers. This group can manage any and all aspects of the Windows NT domain. Initial membership in the Administrators group is granted to the precreated Administrator account and the Domain Admins global group if the Workstation has joined a domain.

The Backup Operators local group's members have the right to back up and restore any files on the system. This right will supersede any permissions assigned to these files and directories. Backup Operators can also shut down a server.

The Guests local group gives members the ability to grant access to specific resources to guests of the domain. Initial membership in the Guests local group is granted to the Domain Guests global group from the domain if there is one.

The Replicator group is used by the Directory Replicator service. Membership in this group allows a member to be involved in the process of maintaining a directory structure and its contents on multiple domain controllers.

The Users local group contains the global group Domain Users if the workstation is a member of a domain. This group is most often used when the security on a Windows NT domain is being increased. Rather than keeping the default share and NTFS permissions, use the local group Users instead of Everyone.

Managing Windows NT User Rights

User rights, as shown in Figure 3.5, are used to define security when the activity to be performed by a user cannot be associated with one particular object. There are several predefined user rights that can grant these nondiscretionary levels of access to the system. The User Rights policy is implemented via Policy | User Manager's User Rights.

Generally, you do not want to adjust the default user rights. If you do change the user rights, the system could be rendered unusable. There are some suggested guidelines to further secure your system's user rights. These are two of the rights that have been granted as default access rights:

- **Log on locally.** The default membership includes the Everyone and Guest groups on Windows NT Workstation. It is recommended that you remove these two groups and replace them with the Users local group from the local account database. Be sure that the domain's Domain Users global group is a member of the Users local group if the workstation is a member of a domain.

- **Shut down the system.** The default membership in Windows NT Workstation includes the Everyone group. This group should not be assigned this privilege. You might also want to consider revoking this right from the Everyone group if you want all systems to be left running during the night.

FIGURE 3.5
The User Rights Policy dialog box.

Administering Account Policies

Before you start implementing user accounts, one of the most important policies to set is your account policy, shown in Figure 3.6.

These policies affect every account on the system—there is no picking and choosing which ones are affected. The account policies define how password changes will be handled and how to react in the case of a user improperly entering her password. You can override these settings through the individual account properties, as mentioned previously.

The password portion of account policy determines your rules for password security. Options within the account policy include the following:

- Maximum Password Age
- Minimum Password Age
- Minimum Password Length
- Password Uniqueness
- Account Lockout
- Lockout Duration
- Handling remote users whose logon hours have expired
- Changing passwords

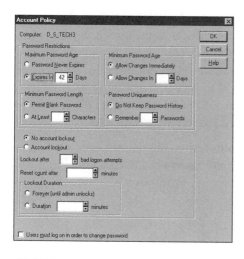

FIGURE 3.6
The Account Policy dialog box and its default settings.

When a maximum password age is used, users get a warning 14 days before the password is set to expire. The default value is 42, but it can be any number of days between 1 and 999.

Minimum password age can also be any number between 1 and 999, and it requires users to keep a password, after having made a change, for the number of days set.

Minimum password length forces users to choose a password of up to 14 characters (although 6 to 8 characters is best for most implementations).

Password uniqueness keeps a history of passwords the user has used and will not let them use a password again for a number of iterations.

At the bottom of the Account Policy screen is configuration information pertinent to unauthorized logon attempts. If this capability is utilized (and it should be), Windows NT will lock out an account after a given number of bad logon attempts. To configure this, you must specify the number of bad attempts that will activate the lockout, how long the system should wait following a bad logon attempt before resetting the counter, and how long the account should stay locked out.

Word of warning: If you choose Forever for the lockout duration, you are increasing the amount of workload for the administrator who must manually reset the account before the user can get back in again.

User Must Log On in Order to Change Password

As a user's password nears expiration, the user is prompted at each logon to change it. The user can ignore this message until the age of the password has expired, at which time he cannot log on until the password is changed. The default is for this field to be blank, meaning that the user is presented with the Change Password dialog box and is not allowed to proceed until he has changed the obsolete password.

If you check this field, users are allowed to change the password only after logging on, and because an expired password cannot be used to log on, the administrator must be summoned from User Manager.

Auditing Changes to the User Account Database

When an organization implements decentralized administration of the Windows NT Account database, it might be desirable to audit all changes to the Accounts database. Remember, only members of the local groups Administrators and Power Users can add, modify, and delete users in User Manager.

To enable auditing of changes to the account database, a member of the Administrators group must enable auditing of User and Group Management, as shown in Figure 3.7. If the objective is to know exactly what files are being updated, File and Object Access should also be enabled.

At the risk of stating the obvious, File and Object Access is a two-step process. The first step is as described previously, but then the administrator must enable auditing of a particular file or directory from the security properties of the file or directory (as stands to reason, only files or directories on NTFS partitions can be audited).

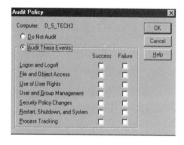

FIGURE 3.7
The Audit Policy dialog box.

The addition of File and Object Access would help you determine if a Power User attempted to add a member to the Administrators group. When this attempt is made, the user faces a dialog box stating that the attempt is unsuccessful. Just auditing User and Group Management would not capture this error. You must enable File and Object Access so that you can see the unsuccessful attempt to write to the SAM database.

CREATING AND MODIFYING USER PROFILES

The use of system policies and user profiles assist in the centralization of management in a Windows NT network. System policies help an administrator implement common Registry settings across the enterprise. User Profiles store the user portion of the Registry. They can be implemented as either *local profiles* or *roaming profiles*. A roaming profile allows users to have the user portion of their configuration follow them wherever they log on to the Windows NT network.

Local Profiles Versus Roaming Profiles

Whenever a user logs on to a system, she creates a local profile on that system. The local profile is implemented as a set of directory structures. This directory structure includes the Desktop folder and the Start Menu folder. The user portion of the Registry is stored in the file NTUSER.DAT. All user-specific information is kept in the \%systemroot%\profiles\<user> directory—for example, Application Data, Favorites, and SendTo.

When a user logs on to the network, her desktop and Start menu are also based on the local system she is logging on to. The desktop will be based on the user's profile directory and the ALL USERS directory. The same is true for the Start Menu directory.

The problem with local profiles is that every workstation that you log on to will have its own version of the local profile. User configuration settings will have to be set at each workstation that the user logs on to.

To overcome this problem, you must implement roaming profiles.

Roaming profiles will have the user portion of the Registry download from a designated system to the system that the user is currently logged on to. Any changes to the settings will be stored in the central location so that they can be retrieved at the next workstation the user logs on to.

Configuring Roaming Profiles in Windows NT

If you want to configure a user account to use a roaming profile, the first thing to do is set the profile path in the User Manager for that account. If you are working with a block of users, the best method is to perform a group property change by first selecting all users you want to have roaming profiles and then selecting User | Properties.

The most common configuration is to have a directory shared with a share name such as profiles. It should allow the local group Users the permission of Full Control. With this share, you can now set the user's profile path to be \\server\share\%username%. The next time the user logs on, his profile information can be saved to this central profile directory. Profiles should be kept on NTFS partitions, because you cannot implement share-level security on FAT subdirectories; it must be implemented through NTFS.

System Policies

System policies help the network administrator restrict what configuration changes the user can perform to his profile. By combining roaming profiles and system policies, the administrator is not able to provide the user a consistent desktop, but he is able to control what the user can do to that desktop. Likewise, the administrator can be assured that the user cannot modify certain settings.

System policies work very much like a merge operation. You can think of system policies as a copy of your Registry. When you log in to the network and the NTCONFIG.POL file exists on the domain controller, it will merge its settings into your Registry, changing your Registry settings as indicated in the system policy. This same action takes place on Windows 95 computers if they find a system policy file called CONFIG.POL.

System policies are implemented via the System Policy Editor, and they can be configured to carry out the following actions:

- Implement defaults for hardware configuration for all computers using the profile or for a specific machine.

- Restrict the changing of specific parameters that affect the hardware configuration of the participating system.

- Set defaults for all users on the areas of their personal settings that they can configure.

- Restrict the user from changing specific areas of their configuration to prevent tampering with the system. An example would be disabling all Registry editing tools for a specific user.

- Apply all defaults and restrictions on a group level rather than just a user level.

The System Policy Editor can also be used to change settings in the Registry of the system that System Policy Editor is being executed on. Many times, it is easier to use the System Policy Editor because it has a better interface for finding common restrictions you might want to place on a Windows NT Workstation.

Implementing System Policies

To create computer, user, and group policies, you must use the System Policy Editor. The System Policy Editor is automatically installed on all domain controllers and can be found in the Administrative Tools group of the Start menu. It is not installed on Workstation, by default, and must be copied from the Server tools or Server CD-ROM.

When you create a new policy file, it will present you with two default icons within the policy:

- **Default Computer.** Used to configure all machine-specific settings. All property changes made within this section will affect the HKEY_LOCAL_MACHINE subtree of the Registry. The default computer item will be used for any client that uses the policy and does not have a specific machine entry created for itself in the policy file.

- **Default User.** Used to specify default policy settings for all users who will be using the policy. The default user setting will affect the HKEY_CURRENT_USER subtree of the Registry. If the user is configured to use a roaming profile, this information will be stored in the user's centralized version of NTUSER.DAT in his profile directory.

Configuring Computer Policies

Computer policies can be configured to lock down common machine settings that will affect all users of a Windows NT system. Common settings that are configured include the following:

- Specifying programs to automatically run at startup of the computer system. These can include virus scans. Opening the System/Run option in the Default Computer Properties allows you to specify this setting.

- Ensuring that all Windows NT clients will have the administrative shares automatically created on startup of these systems. This enhances the ability of the administrator to centrally manage the network. Opening the Windows NT Network/Sharing option in the Default Computer Properties allows you to specify this setting.

- Implementing customized shared folders. These include the Desktop folder, Start Menu folder, Startup folder and Programs folder. These can be set to point to an actual network share location so that multiple machines can have common desktops or Start menus. Opening the Windows NT Shell/Custom shared folders option in the Default Computer Properties allows you to specify this setting.

- Presenting a customized dialog box called the Logon Banner that can be used to inform users of upcoming maintenance to the network or for other network information. Opening the Windows NT System/Logon option in the Default Computer Properties allows you to specify this setting.

- Removing the last logged on user from the Authentication dialog box. With many users having poor passwords, knowing the user's login name can help lead to guessing their password. This is also set in the Windows NT System/Logon option in the Default Computer Properties.

Computer policies can also be implemented on a computer-by-computer basis. Selecting Edit | Add Computer does this. This will add a new icon to the policy with that computer's name.

Configuring User Policies

User policies can also be implemented through the System Policy Editor. These policies will affect the HKEY_CURRENT_USER Registry subtree. Each user will be affected individually if a policy exists by his or her name (otherwise, the settings for Default User are active for everyone).

User policies can also be implemented on a user-by-user basis. To create an individual user policy, select Edit | Add User. When a user logs on, NTCONFIG.POL will be checked to see whether there is a policy for the specific user. If there is not, the default user policy will be used for the login process.

Following are some of the common implementations of user profiles:

♦ You can lock down display properties to prevent users from changing the resolution of their monitors. Display properties can be locked down as a whole or on each individual properties page of display properties. You adjust this setting by using the Control Panel/Display/Restrict Display option of the Default User Properties sheet.

♦ You can set a default color scheme or wallpaper with the Desktop option of the Default User Properties sheet.

♦ If you want to restrict access to portions of the Start menu or desktop, you can do this via the Shell/Restrictions option of the Default User Properties sheet.

♦ If you need to limit what applications can be run at a workstation, you can set this in the System/Restrictions option of the Default User Properties sheet. This option can also be used to prevent the user from modifying the Registry.

♦ You can prevent users from mapping or disconnecting network drives by setting the options in the Windows NT Shell/Restrictions option of the Default User Properties sheet.

The Zero Administration Kit (ZAK) from Microsoft is aimed at reducing the amount of time an administrator spends administering a system. This is accomplished through a strict set of system policies: By reducing what a user can do to a bare minimum, you are reducing what you need to administer as well. A graphical demo is available on the Web at http://www.microsoft.com/windows/platform/info/zakdemo.htm.

By reducing the amount of time administration takes, you—in essence—reduce your Total Cost of Ownership (TCO) for the network. This idea has gained enormous popularity in the past year, and other vendors are coming up with similar approaches—most notably, Novell with its Zero Effort NetWare (ZEN).

Implementing Group Policies

If you need to have user settings affect multiple users, you can implement group policies. Group policies do add another level of complexity to the processing of the policies. Some of the additional considerations include the following:

◆ The System Policy Editor uses global groups for group membership. Appropriate trust relationships must be implemented to see the necessary global groups.

◆ Because a user can belong to multiple global groups, the order in which the groups are processed is very important. One group's settings could be the opposite of another group's. Group order is set with the Options|Group Priority menu option.

If the policies being created apply to Windows 95 clients, you must place a copy of the GROUPPOL.DLL file in the System directory of each of the clients. In the absence of this library, group policies do not function for Windows 95 clients.

Processing Order for System Policies

When a user logs on to a network where system policies have been implemented, the following steps will occur:

1. The user successfully logs on to the network.

2. The user profile is read from the NETLOGON share of the authenticating domain controller.

3. If a predefined policy exists for a user, that policy is merged into the HKEY_CURRENT_USER Registry subtree. The processing then moves to step 6.

4. If no predefined user policy exists, the default user policy is processed.

5. The group priority list is examined. If the user is a member of any of the global groups for which a policy exists, that user is processed according to the group priority order. The priority is ordered from bottom to top of the group priority list. Each of the group policies is applied to the HKEY_CURRENT_USER Registry subtree.

6. The machine policies are determined. If there is a predefined machine policy, that policy is merged with the HKEY_LOCAL_MACHINE Registry subtree. If there is not a predefined machine policy for the system that the user is logging on from, the default machine policy is merged with the HKEY_LOCAL_MACHINE subtree.

SETTING UP SHARED FOLDERS AND PERMISSIONS

At A Glance: Standard Permissions

Permission	Explanation
No Access	Users may not access the directory by any means.
List	Users may not access the directory, although they may view the contents list for the directory.
Read	Users may read data files and execute program files from the directory but may not make changes.
Add	Users may not read or even view the contents of the directory but may write files to the directory.
Add & Read	Users may view and read from the directory and save new files into the directory but may not modify existing files.
Change	Users may view and read from the directory and save new files into the directory, may modify and even delete existing files, may change attributes on the directory, and may even delete the entire directory.
Full Control	Users may view, read, save, modify, or delete the directory and its contents. In addition, users may change permissions on the directory and its contents, even if they do not own the resource. Users can also take ownership at any time.

After your groups have been created in Windows NT, the next step of security is to protect your disk resources. Windows NT has two levels of security for protecting your disk resources:

+ Share permissions

+ NTFS permissions

The management of both sets of permissions will protect your Windows NT system from inappropriate access to your disk resources.

Creating and Sharing Resources

Share-level security allows a Windows NT administrator to protect resources from network users. Not only do shares have a level of security, but they also are used as the entry point into the system for Windows NT users.

There are four explicit Access Through Share (ATS) permissions that can be implemented:

+ **Read.** Allows a user to connect to the resource and run programs. The user also may view any documents that are stored in the share but may not make any changes to the documents.

+ **Change.** Allows a user to connect to a resource and run programs. It also allows the user to create new documents and subfolders, modify existing documents, and delete documents.

+ **Full Control.** Allows the user to do anything he wants in the share. It also allows the user to change the share permissions to affect all users. The Full Control permission generally is not required for most users. Change is sufficient for most day-to-day business needs. The default share permission is Full Control for the group Everyone.

+ **No Access.** This is the most powerful permission. When it is implemented, the user who has been assigned this permission will have no access to that resource. It does not matter what other permissions have been assigned; the No Access permission overrides any other assigned permissions.

Determining Effective Share Permissions

When a user, through group membership, has been assigned varying levels of share permissions, his effective shared permissions are the accumulation of his individual shared permissions.

The only time that this is not the case is when the user or a group that the user belongs to has been assigned the explicit permission of No Access. The No Access permission always takes precedence over any other permissions assigned.

Local groups must be created in the accounts database where the resource is located. If the resource is located on a domain controller, the local group can be created in the domain's accounts database. If the resource is located on a Windows NT Workstation or a Windows NT member server, the local group must be created in that system's accounts database.

Share permission can be set only at the root of a share, and all subdirectories of that share inherit the share's restrictions. For example, a directory is shared as Users and given Full Control to the group Everyone. All subdirectories in the root of the share Users will have Full Control to the group Everyone. The only way to get around this problem is to either share at a lower level and implement security through lower-level shares or use NTFS security.

Implementing NTFS Permissions

At A Glance: NTFS Permissions

Level	Directory Permissions	File Permissions
No Access	None	None
List	RX	Unspecified
Read	RX	RX
Add	WX	Unspecified
Add & Read	RXW	RX
Change	RXWD	RXWD
Full Control	RXWDPO	RXWDPO

NTFS permissions allow you to assign more comprehensive security to your computer system. NTFS permissions are able to protect you at the file level. Share permissions, on the other hand, can be applied only to the directory level. NTFS permissions can affect users logged on locally or across the network to the system where the NTFS permissions are applied. Share permissions are in effect only when the user connects to the resource via the network.

NTFS permissions, when applied at the directory level, can be applied as one of the default assignments shown in Table 3.1.

TABLE 3.1

NTFS DIRECTORY PERMISSIONS

NTFS Permission	Meaning
No Access (none)(none)	Gives the user absolutely no access to the directory or its files. This overrides any other NTFS permissions assigned to the user through other group memberships.
List (RX) (Not Specified)	Allows the user to view the contents of a directory and to navigate to its subdirectories. It does not grant the user access to the files in these directories unless specified in file permissions.
Read (RX) (RX)	Allows the user to navigate the entire directory structure, view the contents of the directory, view the contents of any files in the directory, and execute programs.
Add (WX) (Not Specified)	Allows the user to add new subdirectories and files to the directory. It does not allow the user access to the files within the directory unless specified in other NTFS permissions.
Add & Read (RWX) (RX)	Allows a user to add new files to the directory structure. After the file has been added, the user only has Read Only access to the files. This permission also allows the user to run programs.

continues

TABLE 3.1 continued

NTFS Permission	Meaning
Change (RWXD) (RWXD)	Allows the user to do the most data manipulation. The user may view the contents of directories and files, run programs, modify the contents of data files, and delete files.
Full Control (All) (All)	Gives the user all the abilities of the Change Permission. In addition, the user can change the permissions on that directory or any of its contents. The user also can take ownership of the directory or any of its contents.
Special Directory	Can be set as desired to any combination of (R)ead, (W)rite, E(X)ecute, (D)elete, Change (P)ermissions, and Take (O)wnership.

NTFS permissions can also be applied to individual files in directories. The NTFS file permissions are shown in Table 3.2.

TABLE 3.2

NTFS FILE PERMISSIONS

NTFS Permission	Meaning
No Access (none)	Gives the user absolutely no access to that file. This overrides any other NTFS directory and file permissions assigned to the user through other group memberships.
Read (RX)	Allows the user to view the contents of files but make no changes to the contents. The user can also execute the file if it is a program.
Change (RWXD)	Allows the user to make any editing changes to a data file, including deleting the file.
Full Control (All)	Gives the user all the abilities of the Change Permission. The user may also change the permissions on that file and take ownership of that file if she is not the owner presently.
Special File	Can be set as desired to any combination of (R)ead, (W)rite, E(X)ecute, (D)elete, Change (P)ermissions, and Take (O)wnership.

Determining Effective NTFS Permissions

The determination of NTFS permissions is based on the cumulative NTFS permissions based on group membership. As with share permissions, the only wildcard is the No Access permission. If a user or a local group that the user belongs to is assigned the No Access permission, it does not matter what other permissions are assigned. The user will have no access.

Effects of Moving and Copying on NTFS Permissions

Moving or copying a file to a new directory could change the permissions on an NTFS file. This depends on whether the file is moved or copied and whether the target directory is on the same NTFS volume.

If a file is *copied* from one directory to another on a single NTFS volume, the file inherits the directory permissions for new files of the target directory. If a file is *moved* from one directory to another directory on the same NTFS volume, it retains the same NTFS permissions it had from the originating directory.

Where this gets confusing is in the case of moving or copying files from one NTFS volume to another NTFS volume. When you *copy* a file from one NTFS volume to another NTFS volume, the file always inherits the permissions of the target directory. This is also the case when you *move* a file between NTFS volumes. This is due to the fact that the file is not actually moved between NTFS volumes. The actual process is as described here:

1. The file is copied to the target directory. This causes the file to inherit the permissions of the target directory.

2. The file in the target directory is compared to the originating file and verified to be identical.

3. The original file is deleted from the originating directory.

Setting NTFS Permissions

NTFS permissions are set from the Security page of an NTFS file or directory object. To set NTFS permissions, a user must meet one of the following criteria:

- Be a member of the Administrators local group.
- Be a member of the Power Users local group in a Windows NT Workstation.
- Be assigned the NTFS permission of Change Permission (P) for a directory or file resource.
- Be the owner of a file or directory object. The owner of any object can change the permissions of that object at any time.
- Have the permission to Take Ownership so that the user can become the owner of the file or directory object and change the permissions of that object.

Combining NTFS and Share Permissions

When combining NTFS and share permissions, remember the following tips:

- Users can be assigned only to global groups in the same domain.
- Only global groups from trusted domains can become members of local groups in trusting domains.
- NTFS permissions will be assigned only to local groups in all correct test answers.
- Only NTFS permissions will give you file-level security.

Implementing File-Level Auditing

File-level auditing allows an administrator to review the Security Log to determine who might have created, deleted, or modified a specified file or directory. This can help identify problems in the security model implemented in a domain. To set up file-level auditing, two separate steps are required:

- Enable File and Object Access auditing in the domain's Audit policy.

- Enable the detail of file-level auditing you want to employ on specific file and directory objects on an NTFS volume.

For File and Object Access auditing to be used, a member of the Administrators local group must enable the feature. Administrators and any users or groups that have been assigned the user right to Manage Auditing and Security Log can then set auditing on specific directories and review the security log for audit successes and failures.

To set up auditing on a specific directory or file on an NTFS volume, the person assigned the task of setting up auditing must bring up the properties for that directory or file object. By selecting the Security tab of the object, the person can click the Auditing button to set the auditing levels for that object.

Setting the Permissions to Audit

At the auditing properties sheet of an object's Security properties, the administrator has to set the following items:

- Who are you going to audit?

- What actions are you going to audit?

- Do you want to apply this auditing to files and subfolders?

When determining who you are going to audit, remember that you are more likely to determine who was performing a task by auditing the Everyone group rather than a smaller local group. The Everyone group is preferred when auditing because it includes all users that connect to the network (whether they are known users is not important). If you know that only members of the local group Accounting_Users have access to a folder and its subfolders, it would be fine to audit just this group.

After you have selected who you are going to audit, you must select what actions you are going to audit. Auditing is always based on either successes or failures. Be careful what you choose here. The actions that can be audited for a file or folder directly match the six NTFS permissions. You must choose the correct combination of permissions that are being used to determine who is performing the task that has caused the need for an audit. Remember that if you are trying to determine who has been deleting the General Ledger, you must audit delete successes (because they have been very successful in deleting the file). The actions that can be audited include these:

- By enabling the Read event, you can determine whether an attempt was made to open a file.

- By enabling the Write event, you can determine when a user attempted to modify the contents of a file.

- By enabling the Execute event, you can determine when a user attempted to run a program.

- By enabling the Delete event, you can determine when a user attempted to delete a file object.

- By enabling the Change Permissions event, you can determine when a user tried to change the permissions on a file or directory.

- By enabling the Take Ownership event, you can determine when a user attempted to take ownership of a file or directory object.

After setting the auditing, you can check the Event Viewer's Security Log to determine what type of access users have had to the file or directory that auditing was enabled on.

Effects of Moving and Copying Files on Auditing

As with NTFS permissions, the task of copying and moving files directly affects the auditing on files. If you *copy* a file from one NTFS directory to another NTFS directory, the new copy of the file inherits the auditing set on the target directory.

If you *move* a file from one NTFS directory to another NTFS directory on the same logical volume, the file maintains the same auditing settings it had in the first directory.

If you *move* a file from one NTFS directory to another NTFS directory, but the directories reside on different NTFS logical volumes, the file inherits the audit settings of the new folder. This is because anytime a file is moved between volumes on Windows NT, the actual chain of events is copy, verify, and delete. That is, a copy of the original file is placed in the new directory; this copy is verified against the original copy of the file; and finally, if they match, the original file is deleted.

INSTALLING AND CONFIGURING PRINTERS

Printing architecture has come a long way from the days of DOS-based applications. For the exam, you should understand the steps involved in the NT printing process and how to configure all aspects of a printer in NT.

Printing Architectural Overview

The best way to understand the printing architecture of NT is to look at the steps involved in printing a document. The steps involved in the printing process can be summed up like this:

1. An NT application sends a print job, and Windows NT checks to see whether the version of the printer driver on the client is up-to-date with the version on the print server. If not, Windows NT downloads a new version of the printer driver from the print server to the client.

2. The printer driver sends the data to the client spooler. A remote procedure call is made to the server spooler, in essence sending the data to the server spooler on the print server.

3. The server spooler sends the data to the local print provider.

4. The local print provider passes the data to a print processor that renders it into a format legible to the printing device. If a separator page is used, that is added and sent at the beginning. The local print provider passes the rendered data to the print monitor.

5. The print monitor points the rendered data to the printer port and the printing device.

The important components of these steps are examined in the following sections.

All About Printer Drivers

The printer driver is responsible for generating the data stream that forms a print job. It amounts to two DLLs (Dynamic Link Libraries) and a printer-specific minidriver (akin to a configuration file):

- **The Printer Graphics Driver DLL.** Consists of the rendering or managing portion of the driver; it's always called by the graphics device interface (GDI).

- **The Printer Interface Driver.** Consists of the user interface or configuration management portion of the printer driver; it's used by an administrator to configure a printer.

- **The Characterization File.** Contains all the printer-specific information, such as memory, page protection, soft fonts, graphics resolution, and paper orientation and size. It is needed by the two DLLs whenever they need to gather printer-specific information.

The printer driver is specific to the operating system and the hardware platform; thus you cannot use a Windows 95 printer driver with Windows NT or use an Intel printer driver on an Alpha machine.

The automatic updating of the printer driver on the client is a key component of Windows NT printing. As shown in Figure 3.8, when you first configure a Windows NT printer, the Setup Wizard asks for the operating systems and hardware platforms of all client machines that are going to access the printer. It is the responsibility of the Setup Wizard (and the administrator) then to place the appropriate drivers on the server so that they are available for downloading to clients.

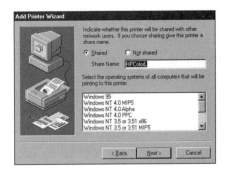

FIGURE 3.8

When you first configure a Windows NT printer, the Setup Wizard asks for the operating systems and hardware platforms of all client machines that will access the printer.

All About the Spooler

The spooler consists of a series of DLLs that accept, process, and distribute print jobs. It operates in the background to manage the whole printing process. All told, the spooler service performs these tasks:

- Keeps track of job destinations

- Keeps track of ports

- Routes print jobs to ports

- Manages printer pools

- Prioritizes print jobs

To function, the Spooler service has to run on both the client and the print server machines. A key point to know for the exam is that the spool file folder, by default, is the winnt_root\system32\spool\PRINTERS directory. This can be changed by using the Advanced tab of the Print Server Properties dialog box, as shown in Figure 3.9 (you can also use Registry Editor to set the spool directory).

The next step in the process involves the print router, for which there is little to say except that it receives the print job from the spooler and routes it to the appropriate print processor.

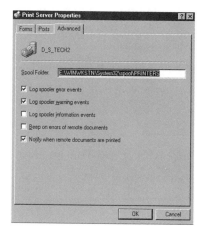

FIGURE 3.9
The Advanced tab of the Print Server Properties dialog box allows you to change the spool location.

All About the Print Processor

Rendering is the process of translating print data into a form that a printing device can read. The printer driver starts the process of rendering, and the print processor completes it. The tasks performed by the print processor differ depending on data type.

The primary Windows NT print processor is called WINPRINT.DLL, and it works with the following:

♦ **RAW data.** Already-rendered data ready for the printer.

♦ **TEXT.** RAW text with very minimal formatting (intended for printing devices that don't directly accept ASCII text).

♦ **EMF (enhanced metafile).** A standard file format in Windows NT and Windows 95 wherein the graphics device interface generates information before spooling. Because the processor, memory, and other resources on the machine are typically beefier than those on the printer, the result is that the control is returned to the user in less time than it takes to wait for the printer directly.

All About Print Monitors

Print monitors control access to specific devices, monitor the status of devices, and communicate with the spooler. The print monitor controls the data stream to printer ports and is responsible for writing a print job to the output destination and taking care of port access.

You install a print monitor by clicking Add Port in the Ports tab of the printer Properties dialog box. Next, click the New Monitor button in the Printer Ports dialog box that appears.

The print monitor can do all the following:

♦ Detect unsolicited errors (such as Out of Paper and Toner Low).

♦ Handle end-of-job notification.

♦ Monitor printer status for printing errors.

The PRINTERS **Folder**

The primary user interface to Windows NT Workstation printing is through the Printers folder. This is available through Control Panel, My Computer, or the Settings item in the Start menu.

> **NOTE**
>
> The Printers folder replaces Print Manager, the printing interface in previous versions of NT.

It is from the Printers folder that you install, configure, administer, and remove printers; watch print queues; pause, purge and restart print jobs; share printers; and set printer defaults.

Printers can be installed on the workstation or through a connection to a remote printer. The remote connection installation is easy to accomplish, whereas installing your own printer is much more involved and requires Administrative or Power User rights.

The installation of both starts with a double-click on the Add Printer icon in the Printers folder to open the Add Printer Wizard, shown in Figure 3.10.

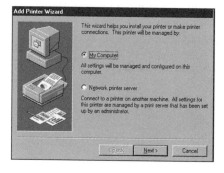

FIGURE 3.10
The Add Printer Wizard.

Adding a Printer on Your Own Machine

As mentioned earlier, to add a printer on your own machine, you must be an Administrator or a Power User. The Wizard begins the process and asks you what port you want to use (as shown in Figure 3.11), and you cannot proceed until you have checked one of the available ports or added a new port.

Next, you must specify the manufacturer and model of the new printer from the list. If you have an unlisted printer, click the Have Disk button and install the driver from a disk.

Next, you must supply a printer name. The only other choice is whether you want the printer to become the default printer for Windows-based programs.

Per Microsoft's recommendations, the printer name can be as long as 32 characters and doesn't have to reflect the name of the driver in use. As with other resources and shares, placing a dollar sign ($) at the end of the share name prevents it from being visible to all other users even though you can choose to share it.

The next choice is if you want to share the printer with other computers on the network. A share name must also be given if you are going to share it (the default is the name from the preceding screen).

If you are sharing, this is the screen at which you must identify the operating systems of computers that will be sharing the printer so that the appropriate printer drivers can be installed.

On completion, the Add Printer Wizard opens the Properties dialog box for the new printer.

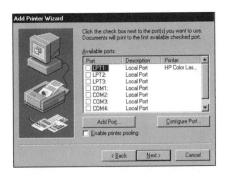

FIGURE 3.11
The Add Printer Wizard first requires that a port be selected.

Adding a Network Print Server

This is a much simpler operation than installing a printer locally. Choosing the network printer server option in the first screen of the Add Printer Wizard opens the Connect to Printer dialog box, which asks for the name of the shared printer to connect to.

Click on the workstation the printer is attached to, and select the printer. To verify settings, the wizard asks whether you want the printer to serve as a default printer, suggests printing a test page, and completes the installation by placing an icon for the printer in the Printers folder.

Configuring Printers

All standard configuration settings for a Windows NT Workstation 4 printer are available through three options of the Printers folder's File menu:

- Document Defaults
- Server Properties
- Properties

Document Defaults

Selecting the printer and then choosing File | Document Defaults opens the Default Document Properties dialog box, shown in Figure 3.12. The dialog box contains document settings for the documents that are to print on the selected printer, and the settings are fairly self-explanatory.

From the Advanced tab, you can change the graphics resolution, color adjustment, print quality, size, source, and orientation settings. The options will vary depending on the print driver installed.

FIGURE 3.12
The Default Document Properties dialog box.

Server Properties

This dialog box, shown in Figure 3.13, contains information specific to the computer's print server activities. To get to it, select the printer and then choose File | Server Properties.

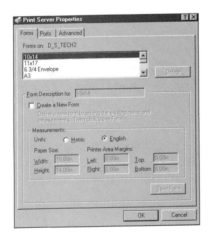

FIGURE 3.13
The Print Server Properties dialog box.

These are the three tabs that appear there:

*   **Forms.** Defines the print forms available on the computer.

*   **Ports.** Maintains a list of available ports. You can add, delete, or configure a port.

> **NOTE**
>
> The Ports tab is the same as the Add Printer Wizard Ports tab except that you don't have to select a port here because you are viewing the available ports and are not associating a port with a particular printer.

*   **Advanced.** Provides the location of the spooler and an assortment of logging and notification options.

Properties

Most configuration settings for a printer are in the printer Properties dialog box. You open this by selecting a printer in the Printers folder, right-clicking, and then choosing Properties. The following sections discuss the six tabs of the printer Properties dialog box.

Printer Properties General Tab

The General tab lets you install a new driver for the printer. There are three buttons on the tab:

*   The Print Test Page button provides a way to test a printer connection.

*   The Separator File lets you choose one of three predefined separator pages or create one of your own. For the exam, it is important to know that NT, by default, does not separate print jobs or use a separator page. The three separator pages that are included with NT are the following:

    *   PCL.SEP: Switches Hewlett-Packard printers to PCL mode.

    *   PSCRIPT.SEP: Switches Hewlett-Packard printers to Post-Script mode.

    *   SYSPRINT.SEP: Is a separator page for PostScript printers.

◆ Print Processor by default is WINPRINT.DLL, but it can be updated or replaced. As mentioned in brief before, WINPRINT.DLL supports five data choices:

• RAW

• RAW (FF appended)

• RAW (FF auto)

• NT EMF 1.003

• TEXT

Printer Properties Ports Tab

The Ports tab lets you choose a port for the printer and add or delete a port. The Configure Port button also lets you specify the Transmission Retry time for all printers that use the same driver.

Printer Properties Scheduling Tab

The Scheduling tab lets you determine when the printer will be available and unavailable and set the printer priority.

NOTE   The printer priority is in no way related to the print job priority.

The priority for a printer defaults to 1 but can be any number between 1 (lowest) and 99 (highest). When more than one printer is printing to the same printing device, it is useful to change priorities (allowing the one with the highest priority to print first).

Printer Properties Sharing Tab

The Sharing tab, shown in Figure 3.14, lets you share the printer with other computers on the network. It is useful if you did not originally install the printer as a shared printer but later decide that you want to share it.

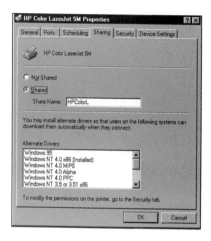

FIGURE 3.14
The printer Properties Sharing tab.

Printer Properties Security Tab

The Security tab lets you configure permissions, auditing, and ownership for the printer. Like all Windows NT objects, printers are protected by the Windows NT security model.

These are the four possible permission levels for printer access:

♦ **No Access.** Completely restricts access to the printer.

♦ **Print.** Allows a user or group to submit a print job and to control the settings and print status for that job.

♦ **Manage Documents.** Allows a user or group to submit a print job and to control the settings and print status for all print jobs.

♦ **Full Control.** Allows a user to submit a print job and to control the settings and print status for all documents as well as for the printer itself. In addition, the user or group may share, stop sharing, change permissions for, and even delete the printer.

A key thing to know and remember is that these permissions affect both local and remote users. By default, permissions on newly created printers are as shown here:

Administrators   Full Control

Creator/Owner   Manage Documents

Everyone   Print

Power Users   Full Control on workstations and servers

You can change the permission level for a group by selecting the group in the Name list and entering the new permission level in the Type of Access combo box, or by opening the Type of Access box. You can add a group or user to the permissions list by clicking the Add button, which causes the Add Users and Groups dialog box to open.

> **NOTE**   The printer Properties Security tab also enables you to set up auditing for the printer and to take ownership of the printer.

Printer Properties Device Settings Tab

The Device Settings tab keeps settings for the printing device. It differs depending on what your printing device is.

Setting Up a Printer Pool

Printer pools are an efficient means of streamlining the printing process in many environments. By its simplest definition, a printer pool is a single logical printer that prints to more than one printing device. It prints jobs sent to it to the first available printing device and provides the throughput of multiple printing devices with the simplicity of a single printer definition. Windows NT ensures that no single device is ever sent more than one document at a time if other devices currently are available. This technique ensures efficient utilization of the printing devices.

Certain criteria must be met before a network can use a printer pool:

- There must be a minimum of two printing devices capable of using the same printer driver. The pool is seen and treated as a single logical device, and thus it must be managed by a single printer driver.

- Though not required, the printing devices should be in close proximity to each other. This is because users have no means of specifying a device within the pool and are given no notification as to which printer actually printed the job. For efficiency, users should not be walking from floor to floor, but rather should be able to check all the printing devices quickly.

You can create a printer pool by configuring the printer to print to more than one port. Naturally, you must also attach a printing device to each port.

MS-DOS–Based Applications

MS-DOS–based applications differ from Windows-based ones in that they provide their own printer drivers. They typically also render data to the RAW data type or to straight ASCII text. Because of this, an application that prints graphics and formatted text must have its own printer driver for the printing device, but the application can print ASCII text without a vendor-supplied printer driver.

> **NOTE**
>
> Most MS-DOS–based applications cannot handle UNC names. Therefore, when printing to a remote printer, you must often map a physical port to the remote printer. This can be done with the command
>
> ```
> NET USE LPTx: \\PSERVER\PRINTER_NAME
> ```
>
> where *x* stands for the parallel port that is to be redirected.

WHAT IS IMPORTANT TO KNOW

The following bullets summarize the chapter and accentuate the key concepts to memorize for the exam:

- SIDs are unique Security Identifiers associated with accounts.
- It is recommended that user and group accounts should *never* be deleted from NT; instead, they should be disabled.
- Two user accounts created when NT Workstation is installed are Administrator and Guest.
- NT Workstation has six built-in groups: Administrators, Backup Operators, Guests, Power Users, Replicator, and Users.
- A global group is a collection of user accounts, and it is powerless by itself. A global group can be created only by a domain controller and is relevant only in a domain environment.
- A local group exists for the purpose of assigning rights and permissions to resources on the machine.
- User Manager is the utility used to create and manage user and group accounts.
- The username is the only value that must be unique for every user.
- The account policy is centered around passwords and applies to the whole system.
- Auditing allows you to track account-related events based on success or failure.
- The %USERNAME% variable can be used to create a unique subdirectory for every user.
- Local profiles are collections of user-specific settings saved on the local machine.
- Roaming profiles are user-specific settings saved on a central server for the purpose of providing the same settings to a user regardless of which workstation that person uses.
- Roaming profiles can be stored on any NT or NetWare server.
- Mandatory profiles prevent users from saving setting changes from one logon to the next.
- Only the Power User or Administrator has permission to create shares in NT Workstation.

- Shared directories can be created from Explorer, My Computer, or the command prompt.

- Access Through Share (ATS) permissions exist whether you are using FAT or NTFS.

- ATS permissions are Change, Read, Full Control, and No Access.

- The NET command is used to create shares from the command prompt.

- You can hide a share by placing a dollar sign ($) at the end of the share name.

- NTFS uses the concept of ownership; FAT does not.

- NTFS permissions include Add, Read, Change, List, Full Control, and No Access.

- NTFS also includes two special permissions: Special Directory Access and Special File Access.

- NT, when using NTFS, can be configured to audit all successful and/or unsuccessful attempts to access an object.

- NT, by default, does not separate print jobs or use a separator page.

- Printer pools are efficient means of streamlining the printing process in many environments.

- MS-DOS–based applications can print ASCII text without a vendor-supplied printer driver, but they need such a printer driver for graphics.

▶ Add and configure the network components of Windows NT Workstation.

▶ Use various methods to access network resources.

▶ Implement Windows NT Workstation as a client in a NetWare environment.

▶ Use various configurations to install Windows NT Workstation as a TCP/IP client.

▶ Configure and install Dial-Up Networking in a given situation.

▶ Configure Microsoft Peer Web Services in a given situation.

CHAPTER 4

Connectivity

ADDING AND CONFIGURING NETWORK COMPONENTS

You can configure all your network components when you first install Windows NT Workstation 4.0. If you want to examine how your network components are configured or make changes to your network configuration, double-click on the Network applet in Control Panel to view the Network properties dialog box. You must be an administrator to make any changes to the network settings on your computer.

Identification Options

Figure 4.1 shows the options available at this tab. Use the Identification tab in the Network properties sheet to view your computer name and your workgroup or domain name. Click the Change button to change your computer name (the maximum length for a computer name is 15 characters) or to join a workgroup or domain (the maximum length for a workgroup or domain name is 15 characters).

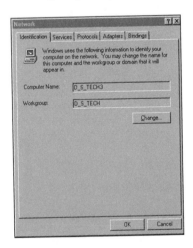

FIGURE 4.1
The Identification tab of Network Services.

The Windows NT security system requires that all Windows NT computers in a domain have accounts. Only domain administrators and other users who have been granted the user right of Add workstations to domain by a domain administrator, can create computer accounts in a Windows NT domain.

If you are a domain administrator, you can give any user or group the user right of Add workstations to domain. Open User Manager for Domains. Choose Policies | User Rights. Make sure that you check the Show Advanced User Rights box.

The following two methods enable you to change your domain name:

♦ If a domain administrator has already created a computer account for your computer, type the domain name into the Domain box and click OK.

♦ Alternatively, you can create your computer account in the domain. To create your own computer accounts, the user name specified must be a domain administrator or have been granted the user right of Add workstations to domain by a domain administrator.

Regardless of which method you use to join a domain, you should see a status message welcoming you to your new domain. You then must restart your computer to complete the process of joining the new domain.

To join a domain, you must have network connectivity to the primary domain controller (PDC) in the domain you want to join. Also, make sure that you do not have a network session open with that PDC. If you must have open network sessions with that PDC, close all open files. Then join that domain, restart your computer, and reopen the files.

Services Options

Use the Services tab in the Network properties sheet to view and modify the network services for your computer. Figure 4.2 shows a standard Services tab.

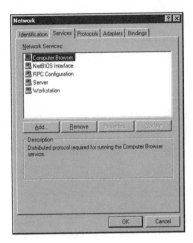

FIGURE 4.2
The Services tab of the Network dialog box.

You might want to add some of the following network services to a Windows NT Workstation 4.0:

- **Client Services for NetWare (CSNW).** Enables you to access files and printers on a NetWare server.

- **Microsoft Peer Web Services.** Installs an Intranet Web server on your computer.

- **Microsoft TCP/IP Printing.** Configures your computer to act as a print server to which TCP/IP-based clients, such as UNIX systems, can submit print jobs.

- **Remote Access Server.** Enables your computer to connect via telephone lines or the Internet to remote networks.

- **SNMP Service.** Enables your computer to transmit status information via TCP/IP to network management stations.

Protocols Options

Use the Protocols tab in the Network properties sheet to view and modify the transport protocols for your computer. Figure 4.3 gives an example of a Protocols tab.

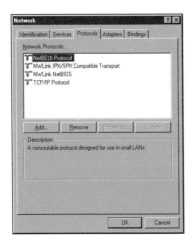

FIGURE 4.3
The Protocols tab of the Network dialog box.

Windows NT Workstation 4.0 allows an unlimited number of network transport protocols. You might want to add some of the following network transport protocols to a Windows NT Workstation 4.0:

- **TCP/IP.** The default protocol for Windows NT Workstation 4.0. It is required for Internet connectivity.

- **NWLink IPX/SPX Compatible Transport.** Required for connectivity to NetWare servers.

- **NetBEUI.** Typically allows connectivity only to other Microsoft-based computers and does not support routing.

You can also add third-party transport protocols compatible with TDI (Transport Driver Interface) and NDIS (Network Device Interface Specification), which have not been developed by Microsoft.

Adapters Options

You can use the Adapters tab in the Network properties sheet to add, remove, view properties of, or update your network adapter drivers. Windows NT Workstation 4.0 allows an unlimited number of network adapters. Figure 4.4 shows the settings for adding an adapter to Workstation.

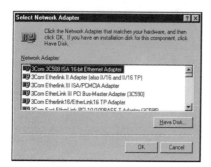

FIGURE 4.4
Adding an adapter through the Adapters tab of the Network dialog box.

NOTE

If you don't have a network adapter, you can still practice installing some of the network services that will not install without a network adapter. Select the MS Loopback Adapter from the Network Adapter list.

Bindings Options

Network bindings are the connections between network services, transport protocols, and adapter card drivers. You can use the Bindings tab in the Network properties sheet to view, enable, disable, and change the order of the bindings on your computer. The current default protocol for each network service appears at the top of each section in the display. The default protocol for the Server service is TCP/IP. Figure 4.5 shows an example of the Bindings tab.

If the binding from the Server service to the NetBEUI protocol has been disabled, client computers that are configured only with the NetBEUI protocol cannot establish network sessions with this computer. This computer can still establish network sessions only with servers configured with the NetBEUI protocol, however, because the Workstation service is still bound to the NetBEUI protocol.

For maximum performance, remove any unnecessary protocols and always make sure that your most frequently used protocol is configured to be your default protocol.

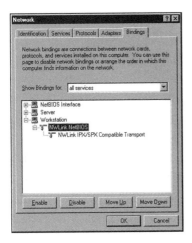

FIGURE 4.5
The Bindings tab of the Network dialog box.

WORKSTATION AS A TCP/IP CLIENT

TCP/IP is the default protocol for Windows NT Workstation 4.0. It consists of a suite of protocols originally designed for the Internet, and as such, it is ideally suited for use with WANs. TCP/IP is supported by most common operating systems and is also required for connectivity to the Internet.

There are two methods by which you can configure TCP/IP information. The first way is to do it manually. Manually configuring, as the name implies, means that all TCP/IP information must be obtained from the network administrator and then entered into the TCP/IP properties section. The problem with this method is that it is very time-consuming, and it leaves a great deal of room for error.

The alternative to manual configuration is to use a DHCP server, which issues configuration information to clients when they need it.

Manual TCP/IP Configuration

When you manually configure a computer as a TCP/IP host, you must enter the appropriate settings, which are required for connectivity with your network. To reach the configuration tabs, choose Network from the Control Panel; then select Protocols and choose the TCP/IP proto-col. Figure 4.6 shows the configuration tabs that appear.

The most common network settings (of which the first two are required) are listed here:

- **IP Address.** This is a logical 32-bit address used to identify a TCP/IP host. Each network adapter configured for TCP/IP must have a unique IP address, such as 192.14.200.4. IP address values are 1-223.0-255.0-255.0-255, with the exception of 127, which cannot be used in the first octet because it is a reserved address.

- **Subnet Mask.** A subnet is a division of a larger network environ-ment typically connected together with routers. Whenever a TCP/IP host tries to communicate with another TCP/IP host, the subnet mask is used to determine whether the other TCP/IP host is on the same network or on a different network. If the other TCP/IP host is on a different network, the message must be sent via a router that connects to the other network. A typical subnet mask is 255.255.255.0. All computers on a given subnet must have the identical subnet mask.

- **Default Gateway (Router).** This optional setting is the address of the router for this subnet that controls communications with all other subnets. If this address is not specified, this TCP/IP host can communicate only with other TCP/IP hosts on its subnet.

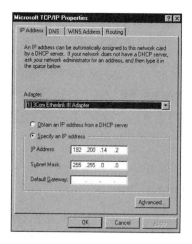

FIGURE 4.6
The IP Address configuration tab.

Domain Name System (DNS) server address settings can also be specified. DNS is an industry-standard distributed database that provides hostname resolution and a hierarchical naming system for identifying TCP/IP hosts on the Internet and on private networks. A DNS address must be specified to enable connectivity with the Internet or with UNIX TCP/IP hosts. You can specify more than one DNS address and the search order that specifies the order in which they should be used.

Windows Internet Name Service (WINS) is similar to DNS, and its settings can also be set here. Computers use IP addresses to identify each other, but users generally find it easier to use other means, such as computer names. Some method must be used to provide *name resolution*, which is the process in which references to computer names are converted into the appropriate IP addresses. WINS provides computer name resolution for Microsoft networks. If your network uses WINS for name resolution, your computer needs to be configured with the IP address of a WINS server (the IP address of a secondary WINS server can also be specified).

Name resolution, in general, is the process of translating user-friendly computer names to IP addresses. If the settings for the TCP/IP protocol are incorrectly specified, you will experience problems that keep your computer from establishing communications with other TCP/IP hosts in your network. In extreme cases, communications on your entire subnet can be disrupted.

Using DHCP for TCP/IP Configuration

Manual configuration of TCP/IP creates a lot of administrative work and is not very efficient. One way to avoid the possible problems of administrative overhead and incorrect settings for the TCP/IP protocol is to set up your network so that all your clients receive their TCP/IP configuration information automatically through Dynamic Host Configuration Protocol (DHCP) servers.

DHCP automatically centralizes and manages the allocation of the TCP/IP settings required for proper network functionality for computers that have been configured as *DHCP clients*. TCP/IP settings that the DHCP client receives from the DHCP server are only *leased* to it and must be periodically renewed. This lease and renewal sequence enables a network administrator to change client TCP/IP settings, if needed.

Configuring DHCP

To configure a computer as a DHCP client, all you must do is select the Obtain an IP address from a DHCP Server option in the TCP/IP properties box.

Testing DHCP

To verify that DHCP is used to obtain your configuration information, choose the Advanced setting from the IP Address tab, and a screen will show that DHCP is enabled.

To determine the network settings that a DHCP server has leased to your computer, type the following command at a command prompt:

```
IPCONFIG /all
```

The following is sample output from the IPCONFIG program:

```
C:\>ipconfig/all:

Windows NT IP Configuration
Host Name . . . . . . . . . : TEST1
DNS Servers . . . . . . . . : 192.14.200.4
Node Type . . . . . . . . . : Hybrid
NetBIOS Scope ID. . . . . . :
IP Routing Enabled. . . . . : No
WINS Proxy Enabled. . . . . : No
NetBIOS Resolution Uses DNS : No
Ethernet adapter CE31:
Description . . . . . . ¬. . : Xircom CE3 10/100 Ethernet Adapter
Physical Address. . . . . . : 00-10-45-81-5A-96
DHCP Enabled. . . . . . . . : Yes
IP Address. . . . . . . . . : 192.200.14.2
Subnet Mask . . . . . . . . : 255.255.255.0
Default Gateway . . . . . . : 192.200.14.1
DHCP Server . . . . . . . . : 192.200.14.16
Primary WINS Server . . . . : 192.200.14.16
Lease Obtained. . . . . . . : Saturday, August 09, 1997 12:31:29 PM
Lease Expires . . . . . . . : Sunday, August 10, 1997 6:31:29 PM
```

Note that IPCONFIG also gives you full details on the duration of your current lease. You can verify whether a DHCP client has connectivity to a DHCP server by releasing the client's IP address and then attempting to lease an IP address. You can conduct this test by typing the following sequence of commands from the DHCP client at a command prompt:

```
IPCONFIG /release
IPCONFIG /renew
```

Static Name Resolution with TCP/IP

DNS and WINS are not the only name resolution methods available for Windows NT Workstation 4.0 TCP/IP hosts—they are only the best. Microsoft also provides for two different lookup files, HOSTS and LMHOSTS, which allow you to use static tables to convert hostnames and NetBIOS names, respectively, to IP addresses. You can find both LMHOSTS and HOSTS in the \winnt_root\SYSTEM32\DRIVERS\ETC folder.

The HOSTS File

The HOSTS file is an ASCII text file that statically maps local and remote hostnames and IP addresses. Prior to NT 4.0 (and still in UNIX and other operating systems), the HOSTS file is case sensitive. With NT 4.0, both Server and Workstation, the file stopped being case sensitive.

The file—in all operating systems and versions—is limited to 255 characters per entry. It is used by PING and other utilities to resolve hostnames locally and remotely. One HOSTS file must reside on each host, and the file is read from top to bottom. As soon as a match is found for a hostname, the file stops being read. For that reason, when there are duplicate entries, the latter ones are always ignored, and the most commonly used names should be near the top of the file.

The following is an example of the default HOSTS file:

```
# Copyright 1993-1995 Microsoft Corp.
#
# This is a sample HOSTS file used by Microsoft TCP/IP for Windows NT.
#
# This file contains the mappings of IP addresses to host names.
# Each entry should be kept on an individual line. The IP address
# should be placed in the first column followed by the corresponding
# host name.The IP address and the host name should be separated by at
# least one space.
#
# Additionally, comments (such as these) may be inserted on individual
# lines or following the machine name denoted by a '#' symbol.
#
# For example:
#
#      102.54.94.97     rhino.acme.com          # source server
#      38.25.63.10      x.acme.com              # x client host

127.0.0.1        localhost
```

You should notice several things in this file. First, the pound sign (#) indicates a comment. When the system reads the file, every line beginning with a comment is ignored. When a # appears in the middle of a line, the line is read only up to the sign. If this file were in use on a live system, you would delete the first 17 lines or move them to the end of the file to keep them from being read every time the file is referenced.

The second thing to note is the following entry:

```
127.0.0.1      localhost
```

This is a *loopback* address in every host. It references the internal card, regardless of the host address, and it can be used for diagnostics to verify that processes are working properly internally before testing whether they are working properly down the wire.

Within the HOSTS file, fields are separated by whitespace that can be tabs or spaces. As mentioned earlier, you can refer to a host by more than one name. To do so, separate the entries on the same line with whitespace, as shown in the following example:

```
127.0.0.1      me loopback localhost
199.9.200.7    SALES7 victor
199.9.200.4    SALES4 nikki
199.9.200.3    SALES3 cole
199.9.200.2    SALES2 victoria
199.9.200.1    SALES1 nicholas
199.9.200.5    SALES5 jack
199.9.200.11   ACCT1
199.9.200.12   ACCT2
199.9.200.13   ACCT3
199.9.200.14   ACCT4
199.9.200.15   ACCT5
199.9.200.17   ACCT7
```

The aliases are other names by which the system can be referred to. Here, me and loopback do the same as localhost, and nicholas is the same as SALES1. If an alias is used more than once, the search stops at the first match because the file is searched from top to bottom.

The LMHOSTS File

Whereas the HOSTS file contains the mappings of IP addresses to hostnames, the LMHOSTS file contains the mappings of IP addresses to Windows NT computer names. When one is speaking of Windows NT computer names, the inference is to NetBIOS names, or the names that would be used in conjunction with NET USE statements.

An example of the default version of this file follows:

```
# Copyright 1993-1995 Microsoft Corp.
#
# This is a sample LMHOSTS file used by the Microsoft TCP/IP for
# WindowsNT.
#
# This file contains the mappings of IP addresses to NT
# computernames (NetBIOS) names.  Each entry should be kept on an
# individual line.The IP address should be placed in the first
# column followed by the corresponding computername. The address and
# the computername should be separated by at least one space or tab.
# The "#" character is generally used to denote the start of a
# comment (see the exceptions below).
#
# This file is compatible with Microsoft LAN Manager 2.x TCP/IP
# lmhosts files and offers the following extensions:
#
#      #PRE
#      #DOM:<domain>
#      #INCLUDE <filename>
#      #BEGIN_ALTERNATE
#      #END_ALTERNATE
#      \0xnn (non-printing character support)
#
# Following any entry in the file with the characters "#PRE" will
# cause the entry to be preloaded into the name cache. By default,
# entries are not preloaded, but are parsed only after dynamic name
# resolution fails.
# Following an entry with the "#DOM:<domain>" tag will associate the
# entry with the domain specified by <domain>. This affects how the
# browser and logon services behave in TCP/IP environments. To
# preload the host name associated with #DOM entry, it is necessary
# to also add a #PRE to the line. The <domain> is always preloaded
# although it will not be shown when the name cache is viewed.
#
# Specifying "#INCLUDE <filename>" will force the RFC NetBIOS (NBT)
# software to seek the specified <filename> and parse it as if it
# were local. <filename> is generally a UNC-based name, allowing a
# centralized lmhosts file to be maintained on a server.
# It is ALWAYS necessary to provide a mapping for the IP address of
# the server prior to the #INCLUDE. This mapping must use the #PRE
# directive. In addition the share "public" in the example below must
# be in the LanManServer list of "NullSessionShares" in order for
# client machines to be able to read the lmhosts file successfully.
# This key is under \machine\system\currentcontrolset\services\
# lanmanserver\parameters\nullsessionshares in the registry. Simply
# add "public" to the list found there.
#
# The #BEGIN_ and #END_ALTERNATE keywords allow multiple #INCLUDE
# statements to be grouped together. Any single successful include
# will cause the group to succeed.
```

```
#
# Finally, non-printing characters can be embedded in mappings by
# first surrounding the NetBIOS name in quotations, then using the
# \0xnn notation to specify a hex value for a non-printing
# character.
#
# The following example illustrates all of these extensions:
#
# 102.54.94.97      rhino    #PRE #DOM:networking    #net group's DC
# 102.54.94.102     "appname \0x14"                 #special app server
# 102.54.94.123     popular #PRE    #source server
# 102.54.94.117     localsrv        #PRE    #needed for the include
#
# #BEGIN_ALTERNATE
# #INCLUDE \\localsrv\public\lmhosts
# #INCLUDE \\rhino\public\lmhosts
# #END_ALTERNATE
#
# In the above example, the "appname" server contains a special
# character in its name, the "popular" and "localsrv" server names
# are preloaded, and the "rhino" server name is specified so it
# can be used to later #INCLUDE a centrally maintained lmhosts
# file if the "localsrv" system is unavailable.
#
# Note that the whole file is parsed including comments on each
# lookup, so keeping the number of comments to a minimum will
# improve performance. Therefore it is not advisable to simply add
# lmhosts file entries onto the end of this file.
```

Once more, the pound sign (#) indicates comments, and because the file is read from top to bottom on each lookup, limiting the size of the comment lines at the beginning of the file is highly recommended.

You can use various special commands in the file to load entries into a name cache that is scanned on each lookup prior to referencing the file. (By default, entries are not preloaded but are parsed only after dynamic name resolution fails.) Using these commands decreases your lookup time and increases system efficiency.

Entries in your LMHOSTS file can be imported into a WINS database if you convert to WINS by clicking the Import LMHOSTS button on the WINS Address configuration screen.

USING VARIOUS METHODS TO ACCESS NETWORK RESOURCES

Windows NT Workstation 4.0 offers different methods of working with network resources—each offering different ways of determining what network resources are available to you and the different types of connections you can make to those network resources.

Universal Naming Convention

The *Universal Naming Convention* (UNC) is a standardized way of specifying a share name on a specific computer. The share names can refer to folders or printers. The UNC path takes the following form: `\\computer_name\share_name`. Commonly, the share names (as with the computer names) are limited to 15 characters in length.

It is important to note that connections made via UNC paths take place immediately and do not require the use of a drive letter. It is also important to note that if a dollar sign (`$`) is placed at the end of a share name, it becomes "hidden" and does not show up in listings, but it can still be accessed by use of the UNC name.

You can also use UNC connections to connect to network printers. For example, `\\ACCTSERVER\ACCTPRINT` is the UNC path to a printer named `ACCTPRINT` on a server named `ACCTSERVER`.

NOTE | Many 16-bit applications do not work with UNC paths. If you need to work with a 16-bit application that doesn't work with UNC paths, you must map a drive letter to the shared folder or connect a port to the network printer.

The limitations on lengths for share names are not a reflection on limitations for long filenames. Rather, they are more a reality due to limitations on NetBIOS names—which can be only 15 characters long and cannot contain embedded blanks (for the exam, that is; in reality, NetBIOS names can contain blanks, but it is not recommended). The actual folder name under Windows NT can still be a long filename, but the share needs to be short. For example, your MYDOCS$ share can be a folder on your desktop workstation named My documents where I keep information on service contracts.

Network Neighborhood

If your Windows NT Workstation 4.0 computer has a network card installed, the Network Neighborhood icon appears on your desktop. When you double-click on the Network Neighborhood icon, the list of all the computers in your workgroup or domain appears. By double-clicking on the Entire Network icon, you can also view all computers connected to your network that are not members of your workgroup or domain.

When you view lists of computers in Network Neighborhood, you are actually viewing a graphical representation of what is called a *browse list*. The browse list is actually maintained by a computer that has been designated as a *Browse Master*. All computers in the network (that have an active Server service) periodically announce their presence to the Browse Master to keep the browse list current.

The Browse Master in a Microsoft network receives periodic broadcasts from all servers on the network and maintains the browse list, which lists all available servers.

Note that Windows 95 computers which are in a workgroup that has the same name as a Windows NT domain display together with the Windows NT computers in the browse list when it is viewed.

The NET VIEW **Command**

You can also access the current browse list from the command prompt by typing NET VIEW. The current browse list is displayed on your screen. A sample browse list looks like this:

```
C:\>net view
Server Name              Remark

------------------------------------------
\\TEST1
\\TEST2
\\TESTPDC
The command completed successfully.
```

The NET USE **Command**

You can assign network resources to drive letters from the command prompt by using the Net Use command and the UNC path of the resource. To connect drive letter X: to a share called Kristin on a server named SERVER1, for example, you would type the following command at a command prompt:

```
Net Use X: \\SERVER1\Kristin
```

You can also use the Net Use command to connect clients to network printers. To connect port Lpt1: to a network printer named HP5 on a server named SERVER1, you would use the following command:

```
Net Use Lpt1: \\SERVER1\HP5
```

To disconnect the network resources, use the Delete, or /d, parameter. For the two examples given, use the following two commands:

```
Net Use X: /d
Net Use Lpt1: /d
```

Other parameters that can be used with Net Use include the following:

/HOME	Connects a user to her home directory.
/PERSISTENT	Controls the use of persistent network connections. The default is the previously used setting.
/USER	Specifies a different username with which the connection is made.

WORKSTATION AS A NETWARE CLIENT

Windows NT Workstation 4.0 can run NetWare connectivity services and access NetWare networks quite easily. Depending on your connections and needs, you might need only install the NWLink protocol. To enable a Windows NT Workstation 4.0 computer to access and share resources on a NetWare server, however, it might be necessary to install additional software besides the NWLink protocol on the Windows NT Workstation 4.0 computers. The type of access you are trying to establish determines whether additional software needs to be installed. NWLink can establish client/server connections but does not provide access to files and printers on NetWare servers.

You install the NWLink protocol by adding it to the protocols loaded on your workstation. To do so, simply select Network from the Control Panel, and choose the Protocols tab.

If you want to be able to access files or printers on a NetWare server, you must go one step further and install the Microsoft Client Service for NetWare, which is included with Windows NT Workstation 4.0. CSNW enables Windows NT Workstation 4.0 to access files and printers at NetWare servers running NetWare 2.15 or later (including NetWare 4.x servers running NDS). CSNW installs an additional network redirector on the workstation.

Windows NT Workstation 4.0 computers that have NWLink and CSNW installed gain the following capabilities:

- ✦ A new network redirector compatible with NetWare Core Protocol (NCP). NCP is the standard Novell protocol for file and print sharing.

- ✦ Long filenames, when the NetWare server is configured to support long filenames.

NOTE   It is important to note that long filename support is automatic in Workstation, but these filenames are not saved on the NetWare server unless you have enabled long filename support there by loading the OS/2 Name Space, OS2.NAM.

- Large Internetwork Protocol (LIP) to automatically negotiate and determine the largest possible frame size to communicate with NetWare servers.

In brief, the Microsoft Client Service for NetWare enables Windows NT Workstation 4.0 to access files and printers on NetWare servers. CSNW is ideal if you have a primarily NetWare-based network with a few NT Workstations. If you have a primarily Windows NT–based network with a few NetWare servers, CSNW is not the best solution. Windows NT Workstation 4.0 can access files and printers on a NetWare server without adding CSNW by connecting through a Windows NT Server configured with Gateway Services for NetWare (GSNW). GSNW can be installed only on Windows NT Server, and this is the best approach to take if you have a few NetWare servers with a mostly NT-based network. It is also best suited for minimal access because all users going through the gateway share one session.

> **NOTE**
> Although NWLink and CSNW enable a Windows NT Workstation 4.0 to access files and printers on a NetWare server running NDS, they do not support administration of NDS trees. They also work in only one direction: Windows NT Workstations are enabled to access files and printers on a NetWare server, but NetWare clients are not enabled to access files and printers on a Windows NT Workstation 4.0.
>
> If you need NetWare clients to be able to access files and printers on a Windows NT 4.0 computer, you must install Microsoft File and Print Services for NetWare (FPNW), available separately from Microsoft, on a Windows NT Server 4.0.

Installing CSNW

You install Client Service for NetWare by selecting the Network applet from the Control Panel and then choosing Services and Workstation. Click the Add button, and a list of available services appears. Choose Client Service for NetWare, and you will see a number of files get loaded (you might even be prompted for the original Windows NT Workstation 4.0 CD or disk). If the service has already been loaded on your machine, an error message appears.

After the service has been installed, you are prompted to reboot the workstation. Upon reboot, a configuration screen like that shown in Figure 4.7 appears. From here you can choose the NetWare server to be automatically connected to at login (and authenticated, as well) and can choose to have the login script run if it exists. If you don't have NWLink already installed, CSNW installs NWLink along with the services automatically.

There are a few other changes to be aware of after you install CSNW. The first is a change in the Services tab of the Network applet. The Network Access Order button allows you to configure which network is your primary network if you are connected to more than one (such as a Windows NT network and a NetWare network). You can change the order to increase your efficiency. The network you access the most should be at the top of the order; the one you access the least should be at the bottom.

You can change the order by using the Move Up and Move Down buttons at the bottom of the frame or by making the same selections from a right-click.

The second change to be aware of after installing CSNW is that a new CSNW program is now listed in the Control Panel. This allows you to configure the connection information as shown in Figure 4.7.

Configuring CSNW

As was pointed out after the reboot described previously, users who log on after a boot receive a prompt to enter the details of their NetWare accounts. Users can enter a preferred server for NetWare 2.15 or above or 3.x, can enter their default trees and context for NDS (the default in NetWare 4.x), or can specify <None> if they do not have NetWare accounts. Each time the same user logs on to that computer, that user automatically connects to the specified NetWare account in addition to the Windows NT account.

Each user is requested to enter the NetWare account information only once. The only way to change each user's recorded NetWare account information is to double-click on the CSNW program in Control Panel. You can also use the CSNW program in Control Panel to modify your print options for NetWare printers—adding form feeds or print banners, for example.

FIGURE 4.7
Upon reboot, you are prompted to enter the NetWare server information.

Even though Windows NT Workstation 4.0 attempts to automatically connect you to your NetWare system, there is no direct linkage between the two account databases. If you change either network password, the other password does not automatically change to match your new network password. Pressing Ctrl+Alt+Del and choosing Change Password offers the option of selecting NetWare or Compatible Network in the Domain field, and from here you can change the NetWare password (on NetWare servers running in bindery mode, you can also use the Setpass utility).

Connecting to NetWare Resources

After you install NWLink and CSNW, you access the NetWare servers in your network using the same methods that you use to connect to any Windows NT Server. You can connect to files and printers on the NetWare servers without any special procedures:

- ◆ **Browsing.** After you install NWLink and CSNW, when you double-click on Network Neighborhood and then double-click on Entire Network, you can choose to browse either the Microsoft Windows Network or the NetWare or Compatible Network.

- ◆ **Map Command.** After you install NWLink and CSNW, right-click on Network Neighborhood and choose Map Network Drive from the menu. You can then assign any drive letter to any shared directory on a NetWare server. You can also accomplish this task by browsing to the appropriate resource, right-clicking, and selecting Map Network Drive.

- **Other Commands.** The Capture, Login, Logout, and Attach commands, all from NetWare, can cause problems if run from NT Workstation. Their functionality is available from other utilities supplied with Workstation; therefore, these four utilities should be avoided to prevent execution failures.

If after you install NWLink and CSNW, you cannot establish connectivity to your NetWare servers, you should check to see what IPX frame type they are configured for. There are actually two different, incompatible versions, 802.2 and 802.3. Windows NT Workstation 4.0 attempts to determine the correct frame type automatically, but you might have to specify the frame type manually to make the connection work.

You can change the frame type by following these steps:

1. Choose Network from the Control Panel.

2. Select the Protocols tab.

3. Highlight the NWLink protocol and click the Properties button.

4. Change from Auto Detect to the correct frame type for your network.

The screen that appears is shown in Figure 4.8.

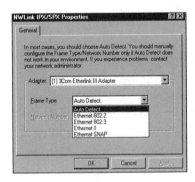

FIGURE 4.8

If connectivity cannot be established, change the frame type to that used by your NetWare network.

CONFIGURING AND INSTALLING DIAL-UP NETWORKING

Remote Access Service (RAS) and Dial-Up Networking (DUN) enable you to extend your network to unlimited locations. RAS servers and DUN clients enable remote clients to make connections to your LAN either via ordinary telephone lines or through higher-speed techniques, such as ISDN or X.25. The incoming connections can also be established via industry-standard Point-to-Point Protocol (PPP) or via the newer Point-to-Point Tunneling Protocol (PPTP) that makes use of the Internet. DUN also supports the use of Serial Line Internet Protocol (SLIP) to initiate dial-up connections with SLIP servers.

You enable Dial-Up Networking services on your workstation by selecting the Dial-Up Networking program from My Computer.

Windows NT Workstation 4.0 is limited to one RAS session at a time, either dial-out or receive. If you need to support more than one simultaneous RAS session, you should purchase Windows NT Server 4.0.

Installing the Dial-Up Networking Client

Installation of DUN can happen when you install Windows NT Workstation 4.0 or later. If you select Remote Access to the network during setup, both RAS and DUN are installed. However, either or both services can be installed separately after installation of Windows NT Workstation 4.0.

To install DUN after installation of Windows NT Workstation 4.0, you must double-click on the Dial-Up Networking icon in My Computer and click on Install to start the Installation Wizard. You then follow the wizard's instructions, shown in Figure 4.9.

During installation, files are copied to the System32 directory, and you will probably be prompted for the installation CD. You will need to specify a minimum of one RAS device, and that can be either a modem or an X.25 device (an ISDN device is also acceptable).

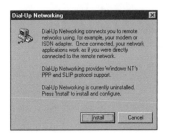

FIGURE 4.9
The Dial-Up Networking Wizard will walk you through the installation
process.

NOTE

If you have a recognizable modem, you will be prompted to use that as the dial-up device. When you click Yes to start the Modem Installer, the Install New Modem Wizard appears.

You can allow the Install New Modem Wizard to automatically detect your modem, or you can select your modem from a list, or you can supply a manufacturer's installation disk. The next step in the installation process is to add the modem as a RAS device. After you add the modem as a RAS device, you must configure it.

After you configure your modem, you must specify how RAS should use the phone line. You have the following options:

- Dial out only (the default setting for Microsoft Windows NT Workstation 4.0)

- Receive calls only

- Dial out and receive calls

You must reboot your workstation to continue with the setup. After the reboot, select Dial-Up Networking from My Computer once more, and you are prompted for location information. After the location information is completed, you can begin adding phonebook entries.

Creating a Phonebook Entry

During the first installation, you are prompted to create a phonebook entry. Following the first time through, you can create new phonebook entries at any time by starting Dial-Up Networking and clicking New. The New Phonebook Entry Wizard then appears, as shown in Figure 4.10.

If you then select the check box labeled I Know all about phonebook entries and would rather edit the properties directly, the New Phonebook Entry property box appears. Each user on a computer has a unique phonebook stored as part of his user profile.

NOTE

If you select manual phonebook entry, the wizard will never bother you again. If you selected this in error and want to be able to use the New Phonebook Entry Wizard again, follow these steps:

1. Double-click on the Dial-Up Networking icon in My Computer.

2. Click on More.

3. Click on User Preferences.

4. Click on the Appearance tab.

5. Click on Use Wizard to create new phonebook entries.

The New Phonebook Entry Wizard automatically starts the next time you run Dial-Up Networking.

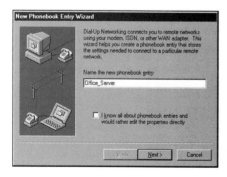

FIGURE 4.10
The New Phonebook Entry Wizard walks you through the steps for creating an entry.

After naming the location you want to connect to, choose the methods by which you are going to connect and the phone number.

Editing Phonebook Entries

After a phonebook entry has been created, you can change the values associated with it by changing any of the three lines of information that appear when the entry comes up, or by clicking the More button, as shown in Figure 4.11.

Choosing the option called Edit entry and modem properties causes five tabs to appear:

- **Basic.** Allows you to change the name of the entry, phone number, or device used.

- **Server.** Allows you to change the line protocol or network protocol used.

- **Script.** Lets you define a script to run upon establishing a connection.

- **Security.** Lets you define the level of security used (discussed in detail in the next section).

- **X.25.** Lets you define the X.25 parameters, if applicable.

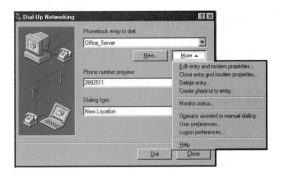

FIGURE 4.11
You can edit phonebook entries by clicking the More button.

Authentication

Security is a major consideration in the design of DUN. From the Configuration tab you can choose from several security settings, including the following:

- **Accept any authentication method including clear text.** Use this setting when you don't care about security.

- **Accept only encrypted authentication.** RAS supports several industry-standard encrypted authentication procedures to support connections to non-Microsoft remote networks. RSA and DES are used to encrypt the data that is passed between the client and server (if this option is enabled). One-time encryption algorithms are used to authenticate the client at dial-up, such as MD2, MD4, MD5, and CHAP.

- **Accept only Microsoft encrypted authentication.** If you select this option, you can also choose to have your entire session with the remote network encrypted, not just your logon. This setting is available only if you are connecting to a Windows NT RAS server.

The authentication and encryption settings are set individually for each phonebook entry.

Changing and Adding Locations

When you double-click on the Telephony applet in Control Panel, the Dialing Properties dialog box appears, as shown in Figure 4.12. You can enter calling-card information by clicking on the Dial using Calling Card check box and then clicking Change.

Line Protocols

The network transport protocols (NetBEUI, NWLink, and TCP/IP) were designed for the characteristics of LANs and are not suitable for use in phone-based connections. To make the network transport protocols function properly in phone-based connections, it is necessary to encapsulate them in a line protocol. Windows NT Workstation 4.0 supports two line protocols: SLIP and PPP. PPTP, an extension of PPP, is also available.

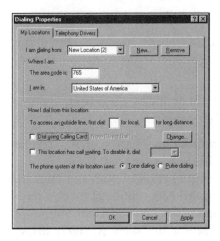

FIGURE 4.12
The Dialing Properties applet lets you change or create new location information.

Serial Line Internet Protocol

SLIP is an industry standard that supports TCP/IP connections made over serial lines. Unfortunately, SLIP has several limitations:

+ Supports TCP/IP only; no support for IPX or NetBEUI.

+ Requires static IP addresses; no support for DHCP.

+ Transmits authentication passwords as clear text; no support for encryption.

+ Usually requires a scripting system for the logon process.

Windows NT Workstation 4.0 supports SLIP client functionality only; operation as a SLIP server is not supported.

Point-to-Point Protocol

The limitations of SLIP prompted the development of a newer industry-standard protocol, Point-to-Point Protocol (PPP). Some of the advantages of PPP include the following:

+ Supports TCP/IP, IPX, NetBEUI, and others.

+ Has support for DHCP or static addresses.

+ Supports encryption for authentication.

+ Doesn't require a scripting system for the logon process.

New to NT Workstation 4.0 is support for PPP multilink, which enables you to combine multiple physical links into one logical connection. A client with two ordinary phone lines and two 28.8Kbps modems, for example, could establish a PPP multilink session with a RAS server with an effective throughput of up to 57.6Kbps. The two modems do not have to be the same type or speed. Both the RAS server and the DUN client must have PPP multilink enabled.

Point-to-Point Tunneling Protocol

New to Windows NT Workstation 4.0 is an extension to PPP called Point-to-Point Tunneling Protocol. PPTP enables clients to connect to remote servers over the Internet.

PPTP enables a DUN client to establish a communications session with a RAS server over the Internet. PPTP enables multiprotocol virtual private networks (VPNs), so remote users can gain secure encrypted access to their corporate networks over the Internet. Because PPTP encapsulates TCP/IP, NWLink, and NetBEUI, it enables the Internet to be used as a backbone for NWLink and NetBEUI.

To use PPTP, first establish a connection from the DUN client to the Internet, and then establish a connection to the RAS server over the Internet.

NOTE

You can also select which of the network transport protocols (TCP/IP, IPX, or NetBEUI) you want to use after you have made a connection to the remote network. The steps to change your RAS configuration after you finish the installation process are listed here:

1. Double-click on the Network program in Control Panel.

2. Click on the Services tab.

3. Double-click on the Remote Access Service in the list.

4. In the Remote Access Setup box:

   ♦ Click Configure to configure port usage.

   ♦ Click Network to select dial-out protocols.

You must restart your computer after you change your RAS configuration.

Whether using PPP or PPTP, after clients establish a connection to a RAS server, they are registered into the local network and can take advantage of the same network services and data that they could if they were actually physically connected to the local network. The only difference that clients could notice is that WAN connections are much slower than a direct physical connection to their LAN.

CONFIGURING PEER WEB SERVICES

Peer Web Services, included with Windows NT Workstation 4.0, is a scaled-down version of Internet Information Server 2.0 (which came with Windows NT Server 4.0). Since the release of NT 4.0, IIS has advanced to version 3.0 and on to 4.0. IIS 4.0 (and likewise, PWS 4.0) no longer resembles 2.0 except in passing. Nevertheless, you need to know the original 2.0 version of Peer Web Services for this exam.

Although PWS is almost identical to IIS, there are several key differences:

- Peer Web Services doesn't support controlling access by IP address. This effectively prevents it from being used as an Internet server where security is a concern.

- Peer Web Services doesn't support virtual servers. This means that it can't be used to host more than one Web site.

- Peer Web Services can't log access to an ODBC datasource. This makes it harder to get statistical numbers on utilization.

- Peer Web Services can't limit the amount of network bandwidth used.

- Peer Web Services has a 40-bit key encryption as opposed to the 40-bit or 128-bit security of IIS. The 128-bit security is available only in the United States and Canada.

- Peer Web Services can't scale by using multiple threads across more than one CPU.

Installing Peer Web Services

Peer Web Services (PWS) is installed from the Services tab in the Network Control Panel applet through the following steps:

1. Start the Network Control Panel applet.

2. Select the Services tab.

3. Click the Add Button.

4. Select the Microsoft Peer Web Services and click OK.

5. Insert the Windows NT CD-ROM as requested.

6. Click OK and reboot the computer as prompted.

After installation, you will see a Start menu group that has the Internet service manager, which can be used to configure Peer Web Services.

Configuring Peer Web Services

The design goal was for PWS to be easy to set up and administer. For that reason, there are only a few options that can even be configured. Following are the most common options, all of which you configure by double-clicking the WWW service in the Internet service manager:

Option	Description
TCP Port	Specifies the port that the Web server will listen to. Web servers are generally located on port 80. This is the default value.
Connection Timeout	Describes how long PWS will keep a connection open that hasn't been closed. The default is 900 seconds.
Maximum Connections	Sets the maximum number of connections that PWS will support. The default value is 100,000. If the clients are accessing the Peer Web server all through the IUSR account,

continues

Option	Description
	NT treats that as a single connection. If the clients are accessing the Peer Web server through their NT accounts, those are treated as separate connections, and the limit is 10.
Anonymous Login	Is the login used by PWS for all connections that aren't specifically logged in.
Password Authentication: Allow Anonymous	Specifies whether PWS should accept connections without requiring logins.
Password Authentication: Basic Clear Text	Allows users to log in via clear text. This is not recommended. Any clear text password can be seen in transit to the server and isn't secure. By default, this option is off.
Password Authentication: Windows NT Challenge/Response	Is a secure form of password transmission that allows users to log in to the PWS server without the password being visible during transmission. By default, this option is on.
Enable Logging	Specifies whether PWS should maintain activity logs. The default is on.
Log Format	Specifies the format of the logging file. You can select NCSA Format or Standard format. Standard format is the default.
Automatically open new log	Specifies the frequency to open a new log. This is useful when you

Option	Description
	want to analyze the data in the log file. If the logs are never closed, you'll never be able to review the information contained in them. The default is daily frequency, but this option can also be set to weekly, monthly, or when the file reaches a certain size.
Enable Default Document	Specifies that PWS will search any directory specified for a certain document, and will send it instead of the directory if the document exists. The default is on, with a default document of DEFAULT.HTM.
Directory Browsing Allowed	Specifies whether PWS should allow the user to see the directory of files for any directory specified. This option is normally turned off to prevent people from finding files that they aren't supposed to. The default is off.

WHAT IS IMPORTANT TO KNOW

The following bullets summarize the chapter and accentuate the key concepts to memorize for the exam:

- The default protocol for Windows NT Workstation 4.0 is TCP/IP.
- An IP address is a unique logical 32-bit address used to identify a TCP/IP host.
- The subnet mask is a value used to determine whether a host is on the same or a different network.
- A default gateway is an optional setting in the TCP/IP configuration that identifies the router used to reach host not on the local network.
- A DNS Server is used for hostname resolution identifying TCP/IP hosts on the Internet.
- WINS is used for IP resolution from NetBIOS names.
- The IPCONFIG utility shows IP configuration information, and the command IPCONFIG /ALL shows all of this information.
- The DHCP service allows IP configuration information to be dynamically leased to client computers.
- Static host and NetBIOS name resolution can be done with the HOSTS and LMHOSTS files, respectively. They are located in the directory \winnt_root\SYSTEM32\DRIVERS\ETC.
- Share names, computer names, and workgroup names are limited to 15 characters in length and often referenced by a UNC name, which takes the form of \\computername\sharename[\optional path].
- Microsoft Client Service for NetWare Networks (CSNW) must be installed with Windows NT Workstation to access files or printers on a NetWare network.
- Microsoft File and Print Services must be installed on an NT 4.0 Server if you need NetWare clients to access files and printers on an NT Server. This is a product available from Microsoft that is not included in the NT core product.
- NCP is the standard Novell protocol for file and print sharing.
- Large Internetwork Protocol (LIP) is used to negotiate and determine the largest frame size that can be used to communicate with a NetWare server.

- If an NT Server is running Gateway Services for NetWare, a workstation client can access the NetWare network through the NT Server.

- 802.2 and 802.3 are the two IPX (NetWare) frame types that CSNW detects.

- Windows NT Workstation 4.0 supports two different line protocols: SLIP and PPP.

- SLIP is an industry standard that supports TCP/IP (and only TCP/IP) connections made over serial lines. Within Workstation, only the client functionality of SLIP is provided.

- PPP supports TCP/IP, NetBEUI, and IPX/SPX, as well as others. PPP also supports DHCP addressing, whereas SLIP does not.

- PPTP, the Point-to-Point Tunneling Protocol, is an extension of PPP that allows clients to connect to remote servers over the Internet and to create virtual private networks (VPNs).

- A Windows NT Workstation is limited to one RAS session at a time. The three settings for it are Dial out only, Receive calls only, and Dial out and Receive calls, of which Dial out only is the default.

- Authentication and encryption settings are set individually for each phonebook entry.

- Peer Web Services (PWS) is a limited version of IIS.

- PWS can't restrict access by IP address.

- PWS doesn't support virtual servers.

- PWS can't create logs to a database.

- PWS can't limit network bandwidth.

- PWS supports only 40-bit Secure Socket Layer (SSL) keys.

- PWS supports all the IIS APIs.

▶ Start applications on Intel and RISC platforms in various operating-system environments.

▶ Start applications at various priorities.

CHAPTER 5

Running Applications

STARTING APPLICATIONS IN VARIOUS ENVIRONMENTS

Windows NT has or has had built-in support for the following:

- 32-bit Windows applications
- 16-bit Windows applications
- DOS applications
- OS/2 1.3 character mode applications
- Portable Operating System Interface based on UNIX (POSIX)

Thirty-two-bit Windows applications are Microsoft's new structure for applications without the memory constraints that 16-bit Windows applications have always had. These 32-bit applications have full access to a more complete API set, have direct access to all of NT's resources, and are the fastest applications that can be run on Windows NT.

POSIX is a source-code-compatible operating environment that allows a single source code to be compiled for multiple systems. The POSIX standard was supposed to revolutionize the way in which UNIX applications were built, reducing the amount of time that must be spent porting an application from one hardware platform to another.

In addition to the two new application standards that Microsoft included, Microsoft enabled Windows NT to run three legacy operating environments.

Sixteen-bit Windows applications were the most popular applications ever written. Windows 3.1 has been—and still is in some cases—deeply ingrained in the workplace. DOS support was also deemed critical to NT's success, and support for it has been included.

Finally, Microsoft included support for OS/2 applications to make it easier for developers and customers to migrate from that platform without feeling deserted and abandoned.

32-Bit Windows Applications

The Win32 subsystem, which all 32-bit Windows applications run from, is the native subsystem for Windows NT and controls all input and output to other subsystems. Thirty-two-bit Windows applications run directly in the Win32 subsystem and have access to the complete system. Each application always runs within its own protected memory space and is preemptively multitasked with other applications running on NT.

Each 32-bit Windows application has the capability to access up to 2GB of memory (the operating system reserves another 2GB). Every application has one thread of execution and can have multiple threads.

A thread is the smallest common denominator a process can be divided into—a string of commands executed in succession. In DOS applications and 16-bit Windows applications, there is only one thread; thus, items are always processed in order, one at a time.

In a multithreaded application, however, one thread can be handling user input while another is printing a document in the background. Because all applications are preemptively multitasked, Windows NT retains control of the system, and even if a single thread locks up, it will not prevent the other threads from running.

16-Bit Windows Applications

Microsoft developed a technique called *thunking* to allow 16-bit applications to run in a 32-bit environment. This is accomplished by converting references (memory addresses) from a 16-bit segmented format to a 32-bit format. Using the thunking method, Microsoft developed a subsystem called WOW (Windows on Windows), or 16-bit Windows on 32-bit Windows.

The WOW subsystem converts 16-bit API calls to 32-bit API calls and handles cooperative multitasking for any 16-bit applications run within it. By default, Windows creates one WOW session when the first 16-bit application is started. This is where all 16-bit Windows applications will be run, unless NT is instructed to start them in a separate memory space (most easily accomplished by checking the check box on the Run dialog box, or on the properties sheet of the application).

When more than one 16-bit application is running in a WOW session, the applications are not protected from each other. The WOW system cooperatively multitasks more than one application in a single WOW session. This means that Windows NT doesn't protect one 16-bit Windows application from having another 16-bit Windows application take up all the WOW session's processor time. In addition, Windows NT doesn't protect an application's memory from being written over by another application.

A tremendous advantage that 16-bit Windows applications have is that they are "binary compatible" and can be run on any platform without having to be recompiled. This is a great feature, but not without its price—every instruction in a 16-bit Windows application will have to be translated to the instruction of the RISC platform, slowing things down immensely.

DOS Applications

As Windows NT does with 16-bit Windows applications, DOS applications have their own translation subsystem that converts 16-bit calls to 32-bit calls. However, this subsystem is rarely referred to separately. In Windows NT, all character-based programs are run from the CMD.EXE program, which is similar to DOS's COMMAND.COM file. CMD.EXE determines whether the command you are running is a 32-bit console application or a DOS application.

If the application is a DOS application, the command spawns a separate NT Virtual Device Manager (NTVDM) session. This is a separate memory space that is protected from the rest of the operating system. Every true DOS application will run on any hardware platform without being recompiled.

OS/2

Microsoft included limited OS/2 support in Windows NT. The limitation is to character-based applications and does not include applications written to use the Presentation Manager interface. OS/2 applications are "source compatible" (like other 32-bit applications) and cannot be run on non-Intel platforms. The only exception to this is that some OS/2 applications (known as bound applications) contain both the OS/2 executable and a DOS executable—they can be run on non-Intel platforms because they can run in DOS mode.

Portable Operating System Interface Based on UNIX (POSIX)

The purpose of POSIX was to reduce the fragmentation in the UNIX market by allowing a single set of source code to run on multiple platforms. It is a C-level source code and API definition required by the federal government for all systems being implemented.

To get NT's full support for POSIX.1, the NTFS file system must be used on all file systems that the POSIX applications are going to access. This allows for the following three components of POSIX systems:

*   *Case-Sensitive Files.* POSIX files are case sensitive.

*   *Hard Links.* The same file can have two different names.

*   *Last Accessed Time.* POSIX requires a last accessed time stamp, which FAT doesn't support. The last accessed time defaults to the last modified time on FAT file systems.

Because POSIX is source compatible only, each POSIX application will need to be compiled for the specific hardware platform on which it will be run.

STARTING APPLICATIONS AT VARIOUS PRIORITIES

One of the key benefits to NT is its task scheduler. The task scheduler for Windows NT determines when each application will run and how long it will be allowed to run. Unlike Windows 3.1, which cooperatively multitasks, Windows NT preemptively multitasks programs.

Cooperative multitasking requires that each application give up the processor after a reasonable amount of time. This works fine when all the applications are well-behaved; however, it doesn't work well when an application doesn't release the processor.

With preemptive multitasking, the operating system maintains control of the processor (or processors) and arbitrates when a program gets to use the processor and for how long.

For a multitasking system to be robust enough to support mission-critical applications and to allow applications to be responsive enough to the user, a somewhat-complex priority scheme must be developed.

Windows NT has just such a complex priority scheme, but it hides the complexities of its scheduling system from you by establishing four priority levels that can be assigned to any program or thread. These are the priorities:

- **LOW.** For applications that need to complete sometime, but that you don't want to interfere with other applications.

- **NORMAL.** For most applications. The default priority.

- **HIGH.** For applications that must complete soon. For use when you don't want other applications to interfere with the application's performance.

- **REALTIME.** For applications that must have the processor's attention to handle time-critical tasks. Applications can be run at a REALTIME priority only by a member of the Administrators group.

These priorities fit within the framework of NT's true numeric scheduling system that has a total of 32 priorities. The following lists the alpha priority and its numeric equivalent:

Alpha Priority	Numeric Equivalent
LOW	4
NORMAL	8
HIGH	13
REALTIME	24

In addition to a process's base priority (what it starts with), NT assigns and schedules from a dynamic (changing) priority. NT decrements and increments a process's dynamic priority from its base priority based on specific circumstances. NT never decrements a dynamic priority to less than the base priority, and it always schedules off of the dynamic priority.

Programs can be started with different priorities through the START command. When a program is already running, the priority can be changed via Task Manager (also discussed in Chapter 6, "Monitoring and Optimization").

The START Command

The START command is a command-line utility that allows you to specify every possible option for starting a program. The START command has the following format:

```
START ["title"] [/Dpath] [/I] [/MIN ¦ /MAX] [/SEPARATE ¦ /SHARED]
[/LOW ¦ /NORMAL ¦ /HIGH ¦ /REALTIME] [/WAIT] [/B] Program [Program
arguments]
```

Of importance here are only the priority options and the /SEPARATE option that starts a 16-bit Windows application in a separate memory space. This will protect it from being interfered with by other errant 16-bit Windows applications. This option is ignored if the application isn't a 16-bit Windows application.

The opposite of /SEPARATE is /SHARED, which starts a 16-bit Windows application in a shared memory space (the default). This option is ignored if the application isn't a 16-bit Windows application.

Task Manager

After a program has been started, there is only one way to change its priority without adding additional utilities—the Task Manager. You can start the Task Manager either by pressing Ctrl+Alt+Delete and selecting Task Manager, or by right-clicking on an open area of the taskbar and selecting Task Manager.

In the Applications tab, all the applications that are running on the system are shown. From this tab you can switch to a task, bring a window to the front, end the application, or go to the main process of the application.

By selecting the Go To Process option from the shortcut menu that you bring up by right-clicking on an application, you are taken to the Processes tab, with the process of the application you picked selected as shown in Figure 5.1.

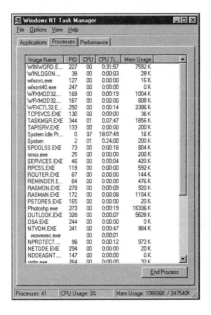

FIGURE 5.1
The Processes tab shows details about the processes, including those that don't
have windows.

By right-clicking on the process, you'll bring up the shortcut menu
shown in Figure 5.2. By selecting the Set Priority option, you have the
ability to change the priority of an application.

If you decide to change the priority of an application, you'll be presented with a warning that changing the priority of an application might
make it unstable. You can generally ignore this option when changing
the priority to LOW, NORMAL, or HIGH, but you should heed this
warning when changing applications to the REALTIME priority.

Task Manager is changing the priority only for that running, and the
next time the process is started, priorities revert to base.

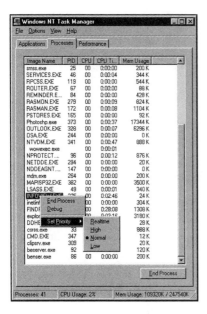

FIGURE 5.2
The Processes tab allows you to change the priority of a process.

WHAT IS IMPORTANT TO KNOW

The following bullets summarize the chapter and accentuate the key concepts to memorize for the exam:

- *Source code compatible* means that the application's source code doesn't need to be modified for the program to run on multiple hardware platforms; however, the program must be recompiled.

- *Binary compatible* means that the program executable can run without modifications on any supported hardware platform.

- Windows NT support OS/2, version 1.3 or lower, character-mode applications on Intel platforms.

- OS/2 2.x+ or OS/2 programs requiring Presentation Manager cannot be run by NT.

- OS/2 "bound" applications have both a DOS version and an OS/2 version in the same executable and therefore can run on any platform.

- DOS applications are binary compatible across platforms.

- 32-bit Windows applications are source compatible across platforms.

- 16-bit Windows applications are run in a WOW (Windows on Windows) subsystem.

- 16-bit Windows applications are not protected from one another and are cooperatively multitasked unless they are run in separate memory spaces.

- 16-bit applications are binary compatible between hardware platforms.

- POSIX applications are source code compatible across platforms.

- Windows NT has four base priorities: LOW, NORMAL, HIGH, and REAL-TIME.

- Only administrators can run applications at the REALTIME priority.

- The START command is used to start an application at a priority other than normal.

- The Task Manager application is used to change the priority of a program that is already running.

- 32-bit applications, OS/2 applications, and POSIX applications can have more than one thread of execution.

- ◆ A thread is a path of execution through the program's code. Each thread is scheduled individually and runs as if it were its own program, but each shares the same memory space as the rest of the threads in a program.

- ◆ Thunking is the process by which 16-bit API calls are converted to 32-bit API calls.

OBJECTIVES

▶ Monitor system performance by using various tools.

▶ Identify and resolve a given performance problem.

▶ Optimize system performance in various areas.

CHAPTER **6**

Monitoring and Optimization

PERFORMANCE TOOLS

Windows NT Workstation includes three primary tools for monitoring system performance:

- Performance Monitor
- Network Monitor
- Task Manager

Performance Monitor

For the most part, Windows NT is self-tuning—one of the design goals that the Windows NT development team was striving for. An excellent utility, *Performance Monitor*, has been included with Windows NT to allow you to see how well your system and its components are running.

Performance Monitor is essentially the same utility that is included in Windows 95, where it is known as System Monitor. It divides components of the system into objects. An *object* represents individual threads, processes, physical devices, and sections of shared memory. Simply put, an object is a mechanism for identifying a system resource.

Objects are then further divided into counters, with each object having a unique set of counters assigned to it. In most cases, objects and their counters are available only when the computer is running the associated software or service. A set of common or core objects can be monitored on any Windows NT 4 system; these are shown in Table 6.1.

TABLE 6.1

CORE OBJECTS CAPABLE OF BEING MONITORED

Core Object Name	Description of Object
Cache	An area of physical memory that holds recently used data.
LogicalDisk	Partitions and other logical views of disk space.
Memory	Physical random access memory used to store code and data.
Objects	Certain system software objects.

Core Object Name	Description of Object
Paging File	File used to back up virtual memory locations to increase memory.
PhysicalDisk	A single spindle-disk unit or RAID device.
Process	Software object that represents a running program.
Processor	Hardware unit (CPU) that executes program instructions.
Redirector	File system that diverts file requests to the network servers. It is also sometimes referred to as the Workstation service.
System	Contains counters that apply to all system hardware and software.
Thread	The part of a process that uses the processor.

When Performance Monitor is started, it begins in Chart view but is monitoring nothing. You must then select, via Edit | Add to Chart, which objects you want to monitor, and which counters to display.

To make your selections, complete the following steps:

1. Use the Add Counter button on the toolbar or the Edit | Add To Chart menu command.

2. Select the Object from the drop-down list.

3. Select the Counter, or select Total for all instances.

To remove items from the chart, select a counter and press the Delete key.

After you've chosen what you want to view, the counters are visually displayed in graph (Chart) view. You can change from graph view to three others:

♦ **Alert.** Allows you to configure intervals to sample an individual counter, and alerts you if thresholds are exceeded. Multiple alerts can be set at one time.

NOTE
For the alerts to be generated from a computer, both the Alerter and the Messenger services must be started.

◆ **Log.** Allows you to log the information (store it in a file for future analysis). At any time, the log file can be opened in Performance Monitor and used to create any of the other three possibilities (a chart, a report, or an alert). When data is currently being logged, it cannot be viewed from another view, and if you try to open the log file, the log is stopped and the counter settings all are cleared. Logs can be used to create base measurements from which your deviations can be noted.

NOTE
If you want to view the contents of the log while it is still collecting data, open a second instance of Performance Monitor. Switch to the desired view (Chart or Report) and set the Data Values Displayed From option to the name of the running log file.

◆ **Report.** Allows you to view the information statistically. It shows the value of the counter, and a report of all the counters can be created.

One key point to remember is that not all the counters are available by default. Certain TCP/IP counters require the implementation of SNMP, whereas other networking ones require the use of Network Monitor Agent.

The physical disk counters appear beneath the physical disk object yet are not turned on by default. This means that although you can choose them, monitoring will show that no activity is occurring. The counters are off by default because keeping track of this information increases the system load by approximately 3% on a 386 machine. The percentage drops below 1% on a 486/33 CPU, and there is virtually no performance loss on a Pentium.

You turn on the counters by going to a command line and typing this:

```
DISKPERF -Y
```

After you reboot, the counters are available for monitoring. When you no longer need to monitor them, turn them off with this command:

```
DISKPERF -N
```

This change also is not active until after you reboot.

The PhysicalDisk object measures the performance of a physical disk, whereas the LogicalDisk object records parameters pertaining to a logical disk (a partition or logical drive that is identified by a drive letter).

PhysicalDisk Counters

The following counters are useful when you're looking for bottlenecks or problems related to the physical disk.

% Disk Time

The % Disk Time reports the percentage of time that the physical disk was busy reading or writing.

Avg. Disk Queue Length

The Avg. Disk Queue Length is the average number of requests for a given disk (both read and write requests).

LogicalDisk Counters

The following counters are useful when you're looking for bottlenecks or problems related to logical disks.

% Disk Time

The % Disk Time reports the percentage of time that the logical disk (C, or D, for example) was busy. To monitor the total activity of all the partitions on a single disk drive, use the % Disk Time counter in PhysicalDisk.

Disk Queue Length

The Disk Queue Length measures the number of read and write requests waiting for the logical disk to become available. Disk performance is suffering if this counter goes above 2.

The Processor Object

There are many counters associated with the processor object. In looking at them, however, be certain to remember that high levels of processor activity can result from two situations other than the handling of a processor-intensive task:

- A severe memory shortage is causing the processor to be busy managing virtual memory (swapping pages of memory to and from the disk).

- The system is busy handling a large number of interrupts.

In either of these cases, replacing the processor with a faster one does not address the real problem, and you must address the true cause.

% Processor Time

The % Processor Time measures the time the processor spent executing a non-idle thread, thus becoming the percent of time the processor was busy. The processor could be a bottleneck if the average value exceeds 80% for sustained periods of time, but occasional spikes are not necessarily indicative of an inadequate processor.

Interrupts/sec

Interrupts/sec measures the number of interrupts the processor handles per second. Hardware failures in I/O devices can be identified by an increase in the number of interrupts.

System: Processor Queue Length

The System: Processor Queue Length measures the number of threads waiting in the queue for an available processor. A number routinely exceeding 2 can indicate a problem with processor performance.

The Memory Object

Symptoms of a memory shortage on a system include a busy processor and a high level of disk activity on the disk holding the page file. The former is indicative of managing virtual memory, whereas the latter is caused by accessing the disk to read and write memory pages.

Pages/sec

Pages/sec measures the number of times that a memory page had to be paged in to memory or out to the disk. An increase in this value over time indicates an increase in paging activity.

Available Bytes

Available Bytes measures the amount of physical memory available. Excessive paging is seen when this value falls below 1MB.

Remote Monitoring

Performance Monitor can be used to monitor computers other than the one whose console you are sitting at. Any computer configured to be remotely administered can be remotely monitored.

To select a remote computer to monitor, type the computer name in the Add Counter dialog box. The person doing the remote monitoring must be a member of the Administrators group of the target computer (in a Windows NT domain environment, the group Domain-Admins is always a member of each workstation's local Administrators group and can remotely monitor the system).

Network Monitor

Network Monitor is a tool that comes in a couple of different formats. One format enables monitoring of the network traffic going in and out of the system running the monitor. A second format permits traffic to be monitored anywhere on the network. Windows NT 4 ships with the version that monitors only the system running the software, whereas SMS (Systems Management Server) includes the Network Monitor capable of monitoring the entire network.

The advantage of the full version of Network Monitor is that any system on the network can be monitored. In addition, Network Monitor can be installed on machines running Windows for Workgroups, Windows 95/98, Windows NT Workstation, or Windows NT Server.

Network Monitor is made up of two components: the Network Monitor application and the Network Monitor Agent. The Network Monitor application enables a system to capture and display network data, display network statistics, and save the captured data for future analysis.

The Network Monitor Agent, on the other hand, enables a computer to capture all network traffic and send it over the network to the computer running the Network Monitor application. This capability is automatically installed on any computer running Network Monitor. It can be run on a Windows 95 system not running the Network Monitor application just to gather network traffic. The information that the Windows 95 system gathers can then be sent to a system running Network Monitor for viewing and analyzing the data. A Network Monitor Agent is available for both Windows 95 and Windows NT. You can also configure the Network Monitor Agent by setting capture and display passwords, as well as by specifying which network card will be monitored if there are multiple cards.

To install the simple version of Network Monitor, do the following:

1. Open Control Panel.

2. Double-click on the Network icon to open the Network dialog box.

3. Select the Services tab and then click Add.

4. Select Network Monitor Tools and Agent, and then click OK until you return to Control Panel.

Task Manager

Task Manager is another tool you can use to see what the system is doing in terms of running applications, CPU statistics, running processes, and memory utilization. You can summon Task Manager by right-clicking on the taskbar, by pressing Ctrl+Alt+Del and choosing it from the menu, or by holding Ctrl+Shift and pressing Esc.

Task Manager has three tabs:

- Applications, from which you can start a new task, switch to a running one, or end a running one.

- Processes, which shows the processes running for the application and the operating system. You can choose to end a process or change its priority.

- Performance, which shows the system performance in terms of processor and memory utilization.

IDENTIFYING AND RESOLVING PERFORMANCE PROBLEMS

Bottlenecks can occur anywhere that resources are limited. Performance Monitor can find bottlenecks by looking at various objects, most of which were described in detail earlier in this chapter:

- **Processor object.** This can identify a shortage of memory (through excessive paging) or determine that the system is busy handling a large number of interrupts.

- **System object.** The Processor Queue Length can show the number of threads in a queue waiting for execution.

- **Memory object.** This shows relevant counters for the system memory.

- **Paging File object.** Important counters here are %Usage and %Usage Peak, which will tell if a paging file is reaching its maximum size.

When you're using Performance Monitor to measure anything, the most important thing to do is establish a baseline. Looking at data once and determining what actions are needed is foolhardy. You must sample data at regular intervals (known as establishing a baseline), see what is occurring over time, and then decide what courses of action need to be undertaken. If you are monitoring multiple performance counters and find the monitoring to be slowing down other operations on your workstation, the best remedy to the situation is to increase the monitoring interval.

Creating a Baseline

An established baseline allows you to compare system performance and see the deviations whenever any changes are made to the system. In the absence of a baseline, you can only guess at the results of any changes (good or bad).

A computer system's baseline is a collection of data that indicates how an individual system resource, a collection of system resources, or the system as a whole performs. This information is then compared to later activity to monitor system usage and system response to usage.

It is important to remember that when setting up the baseline, you should choose the resources to be monitored carefully. Expect demands on a system to increase. Choose all the objects and counters that are important now and that you expect to be in the future. If objects are not chosen in the initial baseline and then become important after the system is put into a production environment, there is nothing to compare data with. Although all systems are unique (very few have identical hardware, software, and services installed), you should always include memory, processor, disk, and network objects in the baseline.

After the initial set of data is captured, use the same settings and capture data on a regular basis. Place this information in a database and analyze the performance of the system. Has it become more efficient? Has it become slower? Are trends developing as more users, more services, or more applications are added to the system? With a good set of data, you should be able to analyze a system and optimize its performance.

To create a baseline measurement, you must use the Log view. This is the only way to create a log of activity. While measuring, you will log, relog, and append logs to get a complete set of information.

As previously mentioned, make an educated choice as to what to select before logging is started. Any kind of analysis should include the four basic objects mentioned earlier. When monitoring a system, however, you might want to include other objects, such as the following:

- Cache

- Logical disk

- Memory

- Network adapter

- Physical disk (if using a RAID system)

- Processor

- System

When relogging, increase the time interval to reduce the file size. In most cases, the extra data that is lost is not critical. As a rule of thumb, you might multiply the time interval by 10. For an initial time interval, you might use 60 seconds. Then when relogging, use a time interval of 600 seconds. For most systems, this approach provides plenty of data.

Another option to consider is to append successive logs to the original log file. This way, all logs are kept together in a "master" log file or archive. No data is lost. To prevent confusion about where one set of data ends and another begins, bookmarks are automatically inserted to separate the logs.

Measurements should be taken for a full week at different times of the day so that information can be recorded at both peak and slack times of each day. As is often mentioned, it is important to record activity during peak periods of the day. It also is important to record activity during slack periods to see just what the level of activity is at those times. Ideally, you should have enough data to know whether there is any significant change in the different counters during different times of the day.

To automate the collection of data, Windows NT 4 is capable of starting Performance Monitor as a service. When started as a service, it has less impact on the system because there is no graphical display that uses valuable resources. To use it as a service, use Performance Monitor to specify the data to be collected. Set the time interval to the desired frequency. Name the log file and save the settings in a Performance

Monitor workspace settings file. Configure Performance Monitor to start as a service when it reboots.

> **NOTE**
>
> Performance Monitor log files can grow to be quite large. Run Performance Monitor on a system that is not itself being monitored and that has a large amount of free disk space. Practice taking logs using different time intervals to get a feel for how large the file will be.

Establishing a Database

The second step in preparing for analysis is to take the collected data and put it into a database so that it can be analyzed. This process involves collecting the information over a period and adding all of it to a database. When in a database, the information can be used to identify bottlenecks and trends. Bottlenecks are the problem areas that needed to be addressed to improve the performance of the system, and trends are useful for capacity planning and preparing for future needs.

After the information is in a database, it is then accessible, measurable, and manageable. The database utilities complement the data collection utilities. The collection utilities gather great quantities of data, and the database utilities enable you to organize the information into meaningful and manageable groups.

Numerous utilities can be used to analyze the data collected. Following are some of the ones Microsoft provides:

- Performance Monitor
- Microsoft Excel
- Microsoft Access
- Microsoft FoxPro
- Microsoft SQL Server

In addition to the utilities listed, many other applications are developed by other vendors.

Regardless of which application is used to analyze the data, the most important step is to collect the data over a significant period.

OPTIMIZING SYSTEM PERFORMANCE

There are various ways to optimize your system, based on what the potential bottleneck might be. Table 6.2 summarizes those that offer the greatest potential gain.

TABLE 6.2

OPTIMIZATION SUGGESTIONS

Item	Considerations
Processor	Upgrade the speed Add another processor Upgrade the secondary cache
Memory	Add more RAM Disable shadowing of ROM BIOS
Disk	Replace slow disks Use NTFS Defragment when necessary Upgrade from IDE to SCSI Isolate I/O-intensive tasks to separate disks Create a stripe set
Network	Get a faster network card Use a faster BUS architecture Upgrade to a faster transfer medium, such as FDDI

Other considerations should include changing the paging file size. The recommended initial paging file size is equal to the amount of RAM plus 12MB. The paging file can be optimized in the Virtual Memory dialog box. To reach this, choose System from the Control Panel; then select the Performance tab and click Change.

Keep in mind that the paging file can be spread across several disks if your hardware supports writing to those disks at the same time and the paging file can be moved to the disk with the lowest activity. In brief, if NT can access a hard disk, NT can place a pagefile on it.

WHAT IS IMPORTANT TO KNOW

The following bullets summarize the chapter and accentuate the key concepts to memorize for the exam:

- The Performance Monitor is Windows NT's all-around tool for monitoring a network using statistical measurements called counters.

- Performance Monitor has the capability to collect data on both hardware and software components. Its primary purpose is to establish a baseline from which everything can be judged.

- Every object has a number of counters. Some to be familiar with are those for the Paging File object—%Usage and %Usage Peak—which will indicate if a paging file is reaching its maximum size.

- To get numerical statistics, use the Report (columnar) view. To see how counters change over a period, use the log feature. To spot abnormalities that occur in data over a period of time, use the Chart view.

- Network Monitor Agent must be installed in order for several of the network performance counters to be available.

- The recommended initial paging file size is equal to the amount of RAM plus 12MB. If the paging file expands beyond its initial size, applications will take longer to start, and the disk that the paging file is on will become more fragmented.

- If paging becomes excessive, the best way to remedy the problem is to install more RAM. If this option is not available, you can also lessen the problem by moving the paging file to a disk that does not contain the Windows NT system files or by distributing it across a number of disks.

OBJECTIVES

▶ Choose the appropriate course of action to take when the installation process fails.

▶ Choose the appropriate course of action to take when the boot process fails.

▶ Choose the appropriate course of action to take when a print job fails.

▶ Choose the appropriate course of action to take when an application fails.

▶ Choose the appropriate course of action to take when a user cannot access a resource.

▶ Modify the Registry using the appropriate tool.

▶ Implement advanced techniques to resolve various problems.

CHAPTER 7

Troubleshooting

WHEN THE INSTALLATION PROCESS FAILS

The Windows NT installation process is remarkably easy for the user, but you still might occasionally experience problems. Microsoft has identified the following common installation problems and solutions:

- **Media errors.** If there seems to be a problem with the Windows NT Installation CD-ROM or floppy disks, ask Microsoft Sales to replace the disk. Call (800) 426-9400.

- **Insufficient disk space.** Delete unnecessary files and folders, compress NTFS partitions, reformat an existing partition or use Setup to create more space, or create a new partition with more space.

- **Nonsupported SCSI adapter.** Boot to a different operating system (one that can use the SCSI adapter) and run WINNT from the installation CD-ROM, try a network installation, and then replace the unsupported adapter with a supported adapter on the Hardware Compatibility List.

- **Failure of dependency service to start.** Verify the protocol and adapter configuration in the Control Panel Network application and make certain that the local computer has a unique name.

- **Inability to connect to the domain controller.** Verify the account name and password, make sure that the domain name is correct, make sure that the primary domain controller is functioning properly, and verify protocol and adapter configuration settings in the Control Panel Network application. If you just finished installing or upgrading, make sure that the domain account for the computer has been reset (added to the network again).

- **Error in assigning the domain name.** Make certain that the domain name isn't identical to some other domain or computer name on the network.

Windows NT can be installed from a network share point or CD-ROM. You need the 3 1/2-inch floppy disks to start the CD installation, but Workstation cannot be installed strictly from floppy disks. To install Workstation 4.0 over a pervious version of Windows NT and keep all settings, install it in the same directory the old version was in. If you install into any other directory, you have not upgraded, but have created a dual-boot machine. Windows 95 cannot be upgraded to Windows NT because there are incompatibilities in the Registry, drivers, and so forth. You must install Windows NT in a separate directory from Windows 95 and reinstall all applications.

Three startup disks are made at the time of installation. If you lose these disks, you can re-create them later by running WINNT /OX.

The error message Cannot Connect to a Domain Controller is one of the more common error messages you might see when you install Windows NT Workstation, change your hardware configuration, or change network settings. There are various explanations for this problem.

N O T E

For the exam, remember a couple of things:

User Manager is used to add users and groups to an NT Workstation. User Manager is a utility that exists only on NT Workstation.

User Manager for Domains is a utility used to add users and groups to a domain. User Manager for Domains is a utility that exists only on NT Server by default. If you install the server tools from an NT Server, then—and only then—User Manager for Domains can exist on an NT Workstation.

Carefully verify that you are entering the correct username and password and that the Caps Lock key is not on. If you are connecting to an NT Server, the first thing you should check is that the account name you are using is listed in the User Manager for Domains on the primary domain controller. An incorrect password generates a different error message than the lack of the user account does.

You should check to see whether the machine account has been added to the User Manager for the primary domain controller. Next, open the Network Control Panel and check that the network bindings are properly installed on the Bindings tab. Some bindings such as TCP/IP require not only computer names, but IP addresses and subnet masks as well. If there is a conflict with two machines on the network having the same IP address, you get an error condition. Failure to enter the subnet mask (or entering an incorrect subnet mask) also prevents your workstation from finding and connecting to a domain controller and getting its network identity properly verified.

WHEN THE BOOT PROCESS FAILS

The key to troubleshooting and solving boot problems lies in understanding the logical sequence the workstation uses when starting. If there is a problem, NT typically shows you various boot sequence errors, the meaning of which should help you determine the problem with your system. You can also examine the BOOT.INI file to determine the nature of any potential problems, and you can apply emergency repair disks to boot your system and repair common boot process failure problems.

The POST Sequence

Your computer begins the operating-system boot sequence after the Power On Self Test (POST) completes. The first messages you see when you turn on the power to your computer are hardware related and are not associated with the boot process. Your memory is tested, for example, and then your bus structure is tested. Your computer runs a series of tests. These tests signal to peripheral devices and sense their replies to check for successful I/O performance. You might see a series of messages regarding the detection of your mouse and keyboard, the appearance of an IDE drive, whether a SCSI adapter is detected, response from any devices on that SCSI chain, and so forth. Failure at this stage isn't a boot sequence problem.

The boot sequence initiates when the hard drive Master Boot Record (MBR) is read into memory and begins to load the different portions of the Windows NT operating system. Windows NT Workstation runs on different microprocessor architectures. The exact boot sequence depends on the type of microprocessor in the system on which you have installed Windows NT Workstation.

The Boot Sequence

Windows NT loads on an Intel ×86 computer by reading a file called the NTLDR or NT Loader into memory from the boot sector of the startup or active partition on your boot drive. The NTLDR is a hidden system file set to be read-only. NTLDR is located in the root folder of your system partition and can be viewed in the Windows NT Explorer when you set the View All File Types option. NTLDR performs the following actions:

- Turns on the 32-bit flat memory model required by the Windows NT kernel to address RAM.

- Turns on the minifile system driver to access the system and boot partitions.

- Displays the Boot Loader menu system on your monitor that provides the operating system to use. These selections are contained in the BOOT.INI file in your system's root directory.

You can install Windows NT Workstation over a previous installation of MS-DOS or Windows 95. These operating systems will appear in the menu and call the BOOTSECT.DOS file when they are loaded and executed. Bootsect.dos loads and hands off at the end of the boot process to the operating-system component responsible for I/O communication. In Windows 95 that file is the IO.SYS file. The following steps round out the boot process:

1. After you select an operating system, a hardware detection routine is initiated. For Windows NT, the NTDETECT.COM program is responsible for this routine, and it creates a hardware list passed to the NTLDR program.

2. The operating system kernel is then loaded. The NTOSKRNL.EXE file located in the %systemroot%\System32 folder is called to load the kernel of Windows NT. The menu is replaced by the OS Loader V4.00 screen.

3. A blue screen appears that loads the Hardware Abstraction Layer (HAL). To execute this, the HAL.DLL is called with a set of routines that isolates operating system functions from I/O.

4. The HKEY_LOCAL_MACHINE\System hive of the Registry is read, and the system is loaded. Registry hives are stored as files in the folder %systemroot%\System32\Config.

5. The boot-time drivers located in HKEY_LOCAL_MACHINE\System\ CurrentControlSet\Control\ServiceGroupOrder are loaded. For each driver that's loaded, a dot is added to the OS Loader screen.

6. The list of supported hardware devices is handed off from
NTDETECT.COM to NTOSKRNL.EXE.

7. After NTOSKRNL.EXE executes, the computer's boot phase finishes and
the software you have installed begins to be loaded.

Because the BOOT.INI file is an ASCII text file, you can edit this file to
control aspects of the boot process. Open the Windows NT Explorer
and remove the read-only and system attributes from the file (which is
located in the %systemroot% top-level folder) before you begin. You will
see that there are two sections to the BOOT.INI, the [boot loader] and
[operating systems] sections, as shown in the following sample:

```
[boot loader]
timeout=30
default=multi(0)disk(0)rdisk(0)partition(1)\WINWKSTN
[operating systems]
multi(0)disk(0)rdisk(0)partition(1)\WINWKSTN="Windows NT Workstation
➡Version 4.00"
multi(0)disk(0)rdisk(0)partition(1)\WINWKSTN="Windows NT Workstation
➡Version 4.00 [VGA mode]" /basevideo /sos
multi(0)disk(0)rdisk(0)partition(1)\WINNT="Windows NT Server Version
➡4.00"
multi(0)disk(0)rdisk(0)partition(1)\WINNT="Windows NT Server Version
➡4.00 [VGA mode]" /basevideo /sos
C:\="Microsoft Windows"
```

You will see parameters that control the time in which a user must decide
on an operating system (timeout), as well as the default location in an
ARC (Advanced RISC Computing) compliant path nomenclature.
There are two ways to change these values, one of which is described
here. The other method, which is much easier, involves changing these
parameters on the Startup/Shutdown tab of the Systems Properties dialog box, which will be discussed momentarily. For now, know that
changing the timeout parameter to 0 makes the boot menu no longer
visible and always boots the default. Making the timeout parameter -1
forces the menu to not count down and always wait for the user to make
a choice.

To change system startup parameters using the System Properties dialog
box, complete the following steps:

1. Right-click on the My Computer icon and choose the Properties
command from the Shortcut menu.

2. Click on the Startup/Shutdown tab of the Systems Properties dialog box if necessary.

3. Select the default operating system desired in the Startup list box from the choices offered.

4. Change the timeout parameter in the Show List for... Seconds spinner.

5. Click the OK button.

The advantage of making changes in the Systems Properties dialog box over manually editing the BOOT.INI file is that any mistake you make when entering information into the BOOT.INI file can cause your system to fail at boot up, whereas the dialog boxes allow you to select only valid choices.

The Load Process

After the boot portion of the operating system loads, your device drivers are loaded and the boot process is handed off to the operating system kernel. In Windows NT, this portion of the startup occurs when the screen turns a blue color and the text shrinks. At that point, the kernel is initializing. The operating system begins to read various hives in the Windows NT Registry. One of the first hives read is the CurrentControlSet, which is copied to the CloneControlSet and from which a HARDWARE key is written to RAM. The System hive is read to determine whether any additional drivers need to be loaded into RAM and initialized. This ends the kernel initialization phase.

The Session Manager then reads the System hive in the Registry to determine which programs are required before Windows NT itself is loaded. Commonly, the AUTOCHK.EXE program (a stripped down version of CHKDSK.EXE) runs and reads the file system. Other programs defined in the HKEY_LOCAL_MACHINE\SYSTEM\CurrentControl Set\Control\Session Manager\BootExecute key are run, and a page file is then created in the location specified in the HKEY_LOCAL_MACHINE\SYSTEM\ CurrentControlSet \Control\Session Manager\Memory Management key.

The Software hive is read, and the Session Manager then loads other required subsystems as defined in the HKEY_LOCAL_MACHINE\SYSTEM\ CurrentControlSet\Control\Session Manager\Subsystems\Required key. This ends the portion of the boot process in which services are loaded into RAM.

After services are loaded, the Windows WIN32 Subsystem starts to load. This is where Windows NT Workstation switches into a graphics (GUI) mode. The WINLOGON module runs, and the Welcome dialog box appears. The Windows operating system is still loading at this point, but the user can enter his username, domain, and password to initiate the logon process. After the Service Controller (SERVICES.EXE) loads and initializes the Computer Browser, Workstation, Server, Spooler, and so on, the request for logon is passed to the domain controller for service.

The SERVICES.EXE program is a central program in the Windows NT operating system. It initializes various system DLL files. If this file is damaged, you must reinstall Windows NT Workstation. The following DLLs provide operating-system services:

- **Alerter** (Alrsvc.dll). Provides messaging services and event alerts.

- **Computer Browser** (Browser.dll). Provides a way for locating resources on the network.

- **EventLog** (Eventlog.dll). Notes and enters events into the three log files.

- **Messenger** (Msgsvc.dll). Provides interapplication communications that enable one application to communicate with another.

- **Net Logon** (Netlogon.dll). Has the code required to request resource validation from domain servers.

- **NT LM Security Support Provider** (Ntmssos.dll). Provides security support.

- **Server** (Srvsvc.dll). Enables Windows NT Workstation to provide limited network services to other computers.

- **TCP/IP NetBIOS Helper** (Lmhsvc.dll). Handles IP address resolution.

- **Workstation** (Wkssvc.dll). Enables a Windows NT Workstation computer to access resources on the network. Workstation includes services that enable the computer to log on to a domain, to connect to shared resources such as printers and directories, and to participate in client/server applications running over the network.

Last Known Good Recovery

A successful logon is considered the completion of the boot process. To mark the event, Windows NT Workstation updates the LastKnownGood control set key in the Registry with information about what was loaded and the current system configuration at startup.

The Last Known Good configuration provides a method for recovering to your preceding system setup. When you create a specific configuration for Windows NT, that information is stored in a particular control set. The LastKnownGood control set enables you to recover from a boot process error—provided that you use this method immediately after discovering the error on the first boot-up attempt and do not log on a second time. Subsequent boots (if they proceed and you log on to the system again) eliminate this option as a recovery method.

The information contained in the LastKnownGood configuration is stored in the Registry in the HKEY_LOCAL_MACHINE\SYSTEM\CurrentControlSet key. To boot to the Last Known Good configuration, follow these steps:

1. Reboot your system.

2. Press the Spacebar when a message appears asking you whether you want to boot the Last Known Good configuration.

3. When the Hardware Profile/Configuration Recovery menu appears, select a hardware profile and press the L key for the Last Known Good configuration.

When a critical system error is encountered, Windows NT Workstation attempts to default to the Last Known Good configuration of its own accord. This defaulting doesn't always occur, but it occurs frequently. If basic operating system files are damaged, you must boot up using a boot floppy disk and recover your system as described in the next few sections.

Boot Sequence Errors

The most common boot sequence errors occur when the operating system components required for the boot process cannot be found or are corrupted. Often a modification of the BOOT.INI file leads to a failure to boot properly. If you have recently made a modification to the startup files, suspect and check that problem first.

Catastrophic hardware failure is not a common problem, but it is encountered—particularly in older equipment. Much less obvious are hardware errors that damage the capability of your system to start without appearing to alter the performance of your system noticeably. If your hard drive develops a bad disk sector that contains the operating system components responsible for booting your computer, for example, the computer appears to function correctly. To solve this problem, you must reestablish the boot files on another portion of your hard drive.

BOOT.INI Error Messages

The following error messages appear when there is a problem with the BOOT.INI file. If you get one of these error messages and the Windows shell doesn't load, you should suspect that the BOOT.INI file is pointing to something no longer valid. If this is the case, you will need to use a boot disk or an Emergency Repair Disk (ERD) to get around the BOOT.INI file. Later in this chapter, you'll learn how to create an ERD.

This message indicates that the Windows NT Loader file is either damaged or corrupted:

```
BOOT: Couldn't find NTLDR
Please insert another disk
```

Typically, the error with the NTLDR file occurs early in the boot process. When you see a repeated sequence of error messages indicating that Windows NT Workstation is checking hardware, the error is a problem with the NTDETECT.COM file. These messages appear as shown here:

```
NTDETECT V1.0 Checking Hardware…
NTDETECT V1.0 Checking Hardware…
NTDETECT V1.0 Checking Hardware…
```

It is possible for Windows NT to load even if the BOOT.INI file is missing. If that is the case, the NTLDR starts Windows NT by loading files it finds in the <default>\WINNT folder. If the operating system was installed in another location, an error message appears indicating that the NTOSKRNL.EXE file is missing or corrupt. The following error message appears when the BOOT.INI file is damaged or when it points to a location that no longer contains the Windows NT Workstation operating system files:

```
Windows NT could not start because the following file is missing or
➥corrupt:
\<winnt root>\system32\ntoskrnl.exe
Please re-install a copy of the above file.
```

This message indicates that the Windows NT operating system kernel has failed to load. The problem most often occurs when someone inadvertently renames the folder containing the operating system files without realizing the consequences of that action. The solution is to use your boot disk to gain access to the system and to rename the folder to the location specified in the BOOT.INI file. It is less common to see a change in the BOOT.INI file giving rise to this problem, because that change requires a knowledgeable user's action.

Other Possible Problems

Another potential explanation for the incapability of the kernel to load could be that you used the Disk Administrator to create a partition with free space. If you changed the partition number that contains your Windows NT operating system files, the pointer in the BOOT.INI file no longer points to the correct location. To fix this problem, you need to edit the pointer to the partition to correct the partition number so that it correctly locates your Windows NT operating system files.

When there is a problem with the boot sector, the following error message appears during startup:

```
I/O Error accessing boot sector file
Multi(0)disk(0)rdisk(0)partition(1):\bootsect.dos
```

This error message might indicate a problem with the BOOTSECT.DOS file. The preceding message is often received in one of two situations: The BOOTSECT.DOS file was deleted, or the partition that the BOOTSECT.DOS file was in was converted to NTFS. You should boot from a boot disk and have the latest disk you created with the RDISK utility handy.

Windows NT Workstation also posts a more specific message when it can determine that the error in locating the boot sector is hardware related. The operating system checks hardware (as you have just seen) by testing it during startup. Failure to respond to one of these tests generates the following message:

```
OS Loader V4.00
Windows NT could not start because of a computer disk hardware
➡configuration problem.
Could not read from the selected boot disk. Check boot path and disk
➡hardware.
Please check the Windows NT™ documentation about hardware disk
➡configuration and your hardware reference manuals for additional
➡information.
```

The preceding message indicates that the pointer in the BOOT.INI file that locates the Windows NT operating system references a damaged or nonexistent device or a partition that doesn't contain a file system Windows NT can access with the boot loader.

Finally, you might see a STOP error if the Windows NT Loader cannot resolve the appropriate partition that contains your operating system files. This error takes the following form:

```
STOP: 0x000007E: Inaccessible Boot Device
```

This error appears when the hard disk controller has difficulty determining which is the boot device—if your computer contains an Adaptec SCSI disk controller, for example, and there is an ID number conflict. Another instance in which this error occurs is when the Master Boot Record is corrupted by a virus or a disk error.

If you have an internal IDE drive on the workstation and a SCSI disk drive with an ID number set to 0, you will also see the inaccessible boot device problem. The 0 ID number is used to specify which disk is the internal disk, and this drive conflicts with a boot partition on the IDE drive. Any bootable SCSI disks can also be booted in preference to your internal IDE drive, so you might want to make all SCSI drives non-bootable to prevent the SCSI disk controller from booting that SCSI drive. (Some disk adapters dynamically assign SCSI device numbers, but they aren't particularly common.) If the Windows NT DETECT program in the boot loader assigns the SCSI bus adapter the number 0, this too makes the reference to your internal IDE drive in the BOOT.INI file inaccurate.

As a general rule, SCSI drives are faster than IDE drives and preferred by the operating system. Don't mix and match these two different drive types. If you have a SCSI disk controller and SCSI drives, locate your boot partition on those.

If your system proceeds through the load phase and boots correctly but still seems to be malfunctioning, you should check the System Event Log to see whether any system messages were written to the log.

The System Log can display errors and warnings, as well as informational events that contain an explanation of the conditions leading to the anomaly you observe due to an error in the boot sequence. Use the Event Viewer program in the Administrative Tools folder on he Program submenu of the Start menu to view the System Log. Choose Log | System Log to open the System log.

Boot Disk Recovery

If your hard disk boot partition fails, you can start up from a floppy disk, provided that you create a Windows NT boot disk before the error condition occurs. If you have installed a multipartition system and your boot partition contains Windows NT, you can also use your boot disk to start up. After you have started your system using the floppy disk drive, you can perform procedures to test and repair any errors that exist.

Most computers are started from their floppy disk drives—commonly given the volume label A. If your computer is set up to start from your hard drive, you must change this in your computer's BIOS setup. Press the keystroke displayed in the startup sequence to open your computer's setup. Then change the boot sequence to start from the floppy disk drive before you attempt to boot from the hard disk.

To create a floppy boot disk, do the following:

1. Insert a blank 1.44MB floppy disk that has been formatted on an NT machine in your floppy disk drive.

2. Double-click on My Computer on your desktop.

3. Right-click on the icon for your floppy disk drive, and then select the Format command from the shortcut menu.

4. Click the OK button to begin the formatting, and then click OK to confirm that the formatting occurred.

5. Select the Windows NT Explorer command from the Programs submenu of the Start menu.

6. Select the BOOT.INI, NTLDR, NTBOOTDD.SYS (optional), and NTDETECT.COM files in the root directory of your hard drive in the Windows NT Explorer. This directory is commonly the c:\ drive.

7. Right-click on any of the selected files and drag them to the icon for your floppy disk drive.

8. Choose the Copy Here command from the shortcut menu.

9. Restart your computer with the boot floppy disk in the floppy disk drive to test the disk.

The Emergency Repair Disk

When a portion of the Windows NT Registry becomes corrupted, your workstation can become unstable and crash. In some instances, these errors even prevent you from starting your computer and booting the Windows NT operating system itself. You can repair the Windows NT Registry by creating an Emergency Repair Disk (ERD) that contains the important system Registry information and using that disk to repair your system configuration.

An ERD contains backup information about your workstation's Security Account Manager (SAM) database, your system configuration, and important system configuration parameters. Also copied to the ERD are the two files required to create a virtual DOS machine (NTVDM): AUTOEXEC.NT and CONFIG.NT.

> **NOTE**
> Use the /s switch to copy over the complete Registry, including the SAM.

You are prompted to create an ERD when you install Windows NT Workstation. If you prefer, you can create an ERD later. Regardless of whether you choose to create an ERD, the appropriate files are copied to the %systemroot%\Repair directory.

If you search for the topic of the emergency repair disk in the online Help system, Windows NT Workstation's Help system steps you through the process of either creating or updating your ERD. You can also open a command prompt window and create or update your ERD by using the RDISK.EXE command. RDISK performs the following functions:

+ Copies the Registry default hive (HKEY_USERS\DEFAULT).
+ Copies the Registry security hive (HKEY_LOCAL_MACHINE\Security).
+ Copies the Registry software hive (HKEY_LOCAL_MACHINE\Software).
+ Copies the Registry system hive (HKEY_LOCAL_MACHINE\System).
+ Copies the workstation SAM.

- Copies the Registry AUTOEXEC.NT file.

- Copies the CONFIG.NT file.

- Copies the SETUP.LOG file. (This contains a list of all the files that were installed during installation. This file is used during the emergency repair process to inspect all the NT files for validity.)

These files are copied into the %systemroot%\REPAIR folder. After these files are copied into the REPAIR folder, the RDISK utility prompts you for a floppy disk on which to create an ERD. The information in the REPAIR folder is copied onto this disk.

The ERD is useful only if you update it on a regular basis. You should consider updating the ERD before any major software installations or upgrades are performed, before any changes to your security policy occur, and before the hardware configuration of your workstation changes.

If this information is not current on your ERD, the restoration you can perform using the ERD is of limited value. The ERD doesn't take the place of a full volume backup; it saves only data that can help reestablish your system configuration based on information contained in the Registry.

Restoring Your System Using the ERD

When you use the ERD to repair a damaged Windows NT Workstation, the procedure essentially reinstalls the sections of the operating system that are required for your particular setup. The data you copied to the ERD contained in the Windows NT Registry determines which files need to be replaced and how the configuration should be reestablished. Among the actions that the ERD performs are the following:

- Runs CHKDSK to determine the validity of the partition containing your Windows NT system files.

- Determines whether the individual files on a system partition are valid, as determined by the use of a checksum.

- Restores missing or corrupt files from your Windows NT installation disks.

♦ Replaces your default system and security Registry hives.

♦ Replaces the Security Account Manager hives.

♦ Reinstalls the files responsible for booting your system in the boot
loader: BOOT.INI, NTLDR, NTBOOTDD.SYS (optional), and NTDETECT.COM.

Preparation Before Restoring

Before you begin to restore your system, make sure that you have your
Windows NT Setup floppy disks handy. If you can't find those disks, you
can create them from the installation CD by using WINNT with the /O or
/OX switch. You can find online documentation for the WINNT.EXE pro-
gram in the Help system. To restore Windows NT Workstation on an
Intel x386 system, complete the following steps:

1. Insert the Windows NT Workstation Setup boot disk into your
floppy disk drive. (Make sure that your system boots from a floppy
disk first to make sure that it will boot at all.)

2. Turn on your system and then insert Setup Disk 2 when asked.
Press the Enter key.

3. Press the R key to perform a repair.

4. Press the Enter key to mark any options you want to restore, press
Tab to move to the Continue button, and press the Enter key
again.

5. Press Enter to detect devices.

6. Insert the Setup Disk 3 into your floppy disk when requested.

7. Insert additional disks with device drives when the Other Disk
option appears, and then replace that (those) disk(s) with Setup
Disk 3 again.

8. Press Enter and insert your ERD when requested, and then press
Enter again.

9. Press Enter to select each Registry hive you want to restore, and
then move to the Continue button and press Enter again.

10. Press the A key to replace all modified system files.

11. Insert any required device driver files requested.

12. Press the Esc key to have Setup ignore the Windows NT Workstation DRVLIB disk, if you want.

13. When the program is complete, reboot your computer.

You can choose from the following four main options to repair in the recovery process:

♦ **Inspect Registry Files.** By using your ERD, you can repair corrupt portions of the Registry. You can select to repair any or all of the following hives: Default, Security/SAM, Software, and System. Changes to the Registry do not require the use of the Windows NT installation CDs.

♦ **Inspect Startup Environment.** Any boot files are inspected, dissected, and potentially rejected. Because all default boot files are equivalent, you can use any ERD to replace startup files.

♦ **Verify Windows NT System Files.** This option compares any system file (with the system attribute) in the Windows NT directory and any subdirectories and verifies them using the checksum values in the SETUP.LOG file. You need your installation disks to perform this repair.

♦ **Inspect Boot Sector.** The most likely reason that the boot sector has become invalid is through the use of the SYS command to upgrade MS-DOS or Windows 95. Use an ERD (any ERD) and the installation disks to repair this problem.

Each ERD you create is specific to the type of computer (vendor and CPU type) on which it is created. An ERD you create on one system does not work on another system.

WHEN A PRINT JOB FAILS

Windows NT enables you to define network printers that are available as shared resources for other Windows NT Workstations to print to. Any client or server on a network can serve as the print server to a network printer. Additionally, you can have local printers that are not shared resources to other network computers but that need to be managed and troubleshot by their owner.

A single standardized print model under Windows replaces the individual print models of applications under MS-DOS. Although this simplifies the process nicely, the down side is that when problems do arise, they affect your entire application suite and maybe an entire workgroup.

Windows still retains the older model for printing for MS-DOS applications that run in Windows NT Workstation from the command prompt. These applications require their own printer drivers to print anything other than ASCII output. If you are using WordPerfect 5.1, for example, both a WordPerfect driver and a printer driver must be installed. Some MS-DOS applications may require that you turn on the printer port by using a command such as the following before printing:

```
NET USE LPT1: \\servername\printername
```

Understanding the Windows Print Subsystem

The printing subsystem is modular and works hand-in-hand with other subsystems to provide printing services. When a printer is a local printer and a print job is specified by an application, data is sent to the Graphics Device Interface (GDI) for rendering into a print job in the printer language of the print device. The GDI is a module between the printing subsystem and the application requesting the printing services. This print job is passed to the spooler, which is a .DLL. The print job is written to disk as a temporary file so that it can survive a power outage or your computer's reboot. Print jobs can be spooled using either the RAW or the EMF printer language.

The client side of the print spooler is WINSPOOL.DRV, and that driver makes a Remote Procedure Call (RPC) to the SPOOLSS.EXE server side of the spooler. When the printer is attached to the same computer, both files are located on the same computer. When the printer is attached to a Windows NT Workstation in a peer-to-peer relationship, those files are located on different computers.

SPOOLSS.EXE calls an API that sends the print job to a route (SPOOLSS.DLL). SPOOLSS.DLL then sends the print job to the computer with the local printer. Finally, the LOCALSPL.DLL library writes the file to disk as a spooled file. At this point, the printer is polled by LOCALSPL.DLL to determine whether the spooled print job is capable of being processed by the printer, and the print job is altered if required.

The print job is then turned over to a separator page processor and despooled to the print monitor. The print device receives the print job and raster image and processes it to a bitmap file that is then sent to the print engine to output.

The Network Printer Process

For network printers, the process is very much the same, but client requests and server services are more clearly defined and separate. The routers found in the spooler modules—WINSPOOL.DRV, SPOOLSS.EXE, and SPOOLSS.DLL—are identical to the ones used for a local printer. A local print provider on the client LOCALSPL.DLL is matched to a remote print provider, WIN32SP.DLL (for Windows print servers) or NWPROVAU.DLL (for NetWare print servers) on the server side. In a network printer process, the print processors and print monitors can use several different server DLLs, each one of which is required by a supported operating system.

Multiple Virtual Printer Setup

You generally install a printer using the Add Printer Wizard that you find in the Printer folder accessed from the Settings submenu of the Start menu. After you step through the wizard, you create a virtual printer with a name that you provide. You can create any number of virtual (or logical, if you will) printers that use the same physical printer for various purposes. If you want to print to a different printer, have different security schemes, or provide different access times, having multiple virtual printers provides a means to do this. You manipulate printers by taking any of the following actions:

- Double-clicking on the printer to see any spooled jobs, provided you have the privilege to do so.

- Right-clicking on a printer to view a shortcut menu that offers several actions. You can use this menu to delete a printer that no longer exists, for example. You can use the Default Printer command to set the default printer for a Windows NT Workstation from the shortcut menu.

♦ Right-clicking on a printer and selecting the Properties command from the shortcut menu to access the Printer Properties and control any number of settings.

Printers As Shared Resources

Network printers are shared resources. You must own the printer (have created or installed it), be an administrator, or be assigned the rights to use a printer in some way to be able to view, modify, and use a printer. Different levels of rights can be assigned by an owner or an administrator. You assign shared rights by using the Sharing command on a printer's shortcut menu, which brings up the Sharing tab of the Printer Properties dialog box.

Creating additional printer shares for the same physical printer proves useful for the following reasons:

♦ Each share can have different printer setups.

♦ It enables you to assign different access privileges to groups of users.

♦ Each "printer" can have different printing priority levels.

♦ You can control access to the printer at different times for each group.

♦ You can use one share for a network printer and another share name for a local printer.

If users cannot see a printer, they might not have been given the right to access that printer. Conversely, if users don't have the right to print to a printer, they should still see it in the Printers folder but should not be able to print to it. An administrator should be able to view and modify printers on any Windows NT Workstation.

If you have MS-DOS clients on the network and you want them to see a printer share, you must use a file-naming convention that DOS recognizes. Names can be up to 12 characters long without spaces or any of the following characters:

? * # | \ / = > < %

To hide a printer share, add a dollar-sign character to the end of the share name, as in *sharename*$. Any printer with that kind of a name will not show up in the Connect To Printer dialog box that is one of the steps in the Add a Printer Wizard. A user must know that this printer share exists and be able to enter both the correct name and the path to the printer share name to connect to that printer.

Solving Print Spooler Problems

Any print job spooled to a printer is written as a temporary file to the `%systemroot%\System32\Spool\Printers` folder. The file is deleted after the printer indicates that the job has been printed. The primary print spool problem encountered is a lack of available disk space. If you print high-resolution graphics, you might have print jobs as large as 20MB to 80MB per file for a 32-bit image at standard page size. Not surprisingly, it doesn't take many print jobs to overwhelm the typical Windows NT Workstation configuration.

When you print to the spooler, you create two files for each print job. The `.SPL` file is the actual print job spool file. You also create a shadow file, which is given the `.SHD` extension. The shadow file contains additional information about the print job that is not part of the print job itself, such as owner and priority. If your computer crashes, `.SPL` and `.SHD` files remain in the default spool file until the service restarts and they are processed and printed. After being printed, these files are deleted from disk. If your spooled files become corrupted, they will be orphaned and will remain in the spool folder, taking up valuable space.

You can print directly to a printer from your application by turning off the print spooling feature. Before you print, open the Scheduling tab of the Printer Properties dialog box and select the Print directly to the printer radio button. When the printer next becomes available, your document prints. Until that point, you cannot use the application that is originating the print job. You can task-switch to another application and continue working until your printing application becomes available.

When all else fails, stop and restart the printer spooler service. This effectively shuts it down and restarts it, thus clearing anything that might have been hung.

Spooler Performance Problems

You can solve spooler performance problems by increasing the priority that Windows NT Workstation assigns to the Spooler service. By default, Windows NT assigns this service a rating of 7, which is consistent with other background processes that run. Increase the rating to 9 to improve the performance of the spooler to the level of a foreground operation. Consider doing this only as a temporary measure to print a large print job or if your workstation is used heavily as a print server. Permanently changing this rating degrades the performance of other services and applications on that workstation.

To change the priority of the Spooler service, open either the RegEdit or the RegEdt32 application and change the value of the PriorityClass of type REG_DWORD in the following key:

```
HKEY_LOCAL_MACHINE\System\CurrentControlSet\Control\Print
```

Set that value to the priority class required. A value of 0, or no value entered, is substituted with the default value of a background process of 7 for Windows NT Workstation. (For Windows NT Server background processes, take a value of 9.)

Aside from changing priority classes, another simple and effective procedure that improves printer performance is defragmenting your hard drive regularly.

Changing the Default Spool Folder

If you run out of room on your system partition for spooled print jobs, you can specify a different default spool folder. To do so, make the change in the Advanced tab of the Server Properties dialog box. Open that dialog box by double-clicking on the Server Control Panel. To change the location of spooled documents, complete the following steps:

1. Create a new spool directory.

2. Choose the Printers command from the Settings menu of the Start menu.

3. Choose the File | Server Properties menu command.

4. Click on the Advanced tab, and then enter the location of the spool file directory.

5. Click the OK button.

Some possibilities to consider include creating the spool folder on an NTFS volume and setting security for this folder. You can also edit the Registry to change the value of the `DefaultSpoolDirectory` of type `REG_SZ`. The path is entered into the following key of the Registry:

```
HKEY_LOCAL_MACHINE\System\CurrentControlSet\Control\Print\Printers
```

After you enter the new folder and its path, save the change and restart your machine for the change to take effect. Any spooled job in the original location will be lost but will not be deleted. You need to delete the `TEMP` file manually.

If you want to have individual spooled folders for each virtual printer, you can assign them. Find your printers in the following key:

```
HKEY_LOCAL_MACHINE\System\CurrentControlSet\Control\Print\~Printers\
printername
```

Then enter the folder and its path as the data in the `SpoolDirectory` value for that key. Again, you need to restart the workstation to effect the change.

Enabling Printer Logging

You can enable event logging to your spooler by adding a check mark to the Log spooler error events, Log spooler warning events, and/or Log spooler information events check boxes on the Advanced tab.

To turn on auditing of a printer share, complete the following steps:

1. Enable File and Object Access auditing in the User Manager.

2. Enable printer auditing for a specific printer share. Open the Security tab of the Printer Properties dialog box and click the Auditing button.

3. In the Printer Auditing dialog box, click the Add button.

4. In the Add Users and Groups dialog box, select a group or user to be audited.

5. Click the OK button to return to the Printer Auditing dialog box.

6. Select a user or group and click on the check boxes in the Events to Audit section to track events you want to log for that user and group.

7. Click OK.

Use the Event Viewer utility in the Administrative Tools folder to view logged events.

Installing Print Pooling

If you have adequate printer resources and want to distribute the print queue load, you might want to install printer pooling. Printer pooling enables you to take two or more *identical* printers and print to them as if they were a single printer. The print job goes to the first available printer and is managed as if it were a single print queue.

To use printer pooling, complete the following steps:

1. Choose the Printers command from the Settings submenu of the Start menu.

2. Right-click on a printer icon and select the Properties command.

3. Click on the Ports tab and select the logical printer to which you want to print.

4. Click on the Enable Print Pooling check box, and then close the Printer Properties dialog box.

To set up a logical printer, you can use the Add Printer Wizard to add a printer to a port and use the existing share name. Although the printers need to be identical, the ports do not. You can mix and match local, serial, and parallel ports for the same logical printer.

Scheduling a Print Job

You cannot specify when a particular job will print on a printer within the current Windows NT Workstation architecture. You can control when a printer is available for printing, however, as part of a printer's definition. Use two differently named printer shares for the same printer, and make sure one printer always is available. Restrict the availability of the second printer, and then use that printer share to schedule your print job.

To set availability times, complete the following steps:

1. Click on the printer icon in the Printers folder and press Alt+Enter to open the Printer Properties dialog box.

2. Click on the Scheduling tab of the Printer Properties dialog box.

3. Click on the From radio button in the Available section, and then enter the starting and ending times when the printer is available.

Any print job printed off-hours is left in the print queue until the printer becomes available.

Using the Print Troubleshooter

To aid in solving printer problems, Windows NT comes with an interactive print troubleshooting aid as part of the online Help system. To access the Print Troubleshooter, complete the following steps:

1. Choose the Help command from the Start menu.

2. Click on the Index tab and enter the keyword `troubleshooting` into the text box.

3. Double-click on the problem type and follow the instructions in the Help system.

Printers are among the most important network resources in many organizations. Therefore, you will be called on often to solve problems that crop up with printer shares and printer hardware. This section reviewed some of the most common problems.

WHEN AN APPLICATION FAILS

Unlike in MS-DOS and earlier versions of Windows, an application failure won't bring your system to a complete halt. Most application failures are recoverable, and in many cases you won't even need to reboot your computer to reestablish a working configuration. That is not to say that a system crash is impossible. It happens very infrequently.

Most often the worst culprits are applications written for MS-DOS or 16-bit Windows applications. These programs tend to crash more frequently than do 32-bit Windows applications—a good reason to upgrade.

If you have a malfunctioning application, bring up the Task Manager and close down the process. You can access the Task Manager by using either your mouse or your keyboard (useful in case either is hung up by a malfunction). To use your keyboard to close an application, complete the following steps:

1. Press Ctrl+Alt+Delete to open the Windows NT Security dialog box.

2. Click the Task Manager button there to open the Task Manager.

3. Click on the Applications tab.

4. Select the offending application and click the End Task button.

5. Close the Task Manager.

You can also open the Task Manager by moving the cursor over an open area of the taskbar, right-clicking, and then selecting the Task Manager command.

If you need to end a 16-bit Windows application or an MS-DOS application, you must close the entire session. When you close a 32-bit Windows application, only the individual process or thread needs to be closed.

Using the Application Log

Many errors are logged into the Application log for native Windows NT applications. The developer of the application determines the events that are logged, their codes, and their meanings. Often an application's manual or online Help system documents the events you see in the Application log, as well as your ability to control the events that are noted.

Service Failures

Many applications run as services on Windows NT Workstation. Internet Information Server's three applications, WWW, FTP, and Gopher, for example, all are services. Services are started, stopped, and paused either from within their central administrative tool (for IIS that tool is the Internet Service Manager) or from within the Services Control Panel. If you want to configure a service so that it runs automatically when your workstation boots, more often than not you will set this behavior in the Services Control Panel.

Sooner or later, sad to say, you will see the following command and infamous error message when your Windows NT Workstation starts up after the load phase:

```
One or more services failed to start. Please see the Event Viewer
for details.
```

The Event Viewer can be used to examine the System log (the one it opens by default).

Use the Event heading in the Event Viewer and look for the Event code that has a value of `6005`. That event is an informational message that indicates the EventLog service has started up. Any event before that is a boot event and should be resolved. To get more information on the event, choose View | Detail, or select the event and press Enter, or double-click on the event message to view an Event Detail dialog box.

WHEN A USER CANNOT ACCESS A RESOURCE

Windows NT's security system controls access to network resources through user and machine accounts. Your logon to a particular domain is validated by a domain controller, and it provides you with certain privileges and rights that are registered in the Security Account Manager database.

When you log on to Windows NT, the system provides a Security Access Token (SAT) based on your username and password. This SAT is a key that enables you to access objects that Windows NT manages by maintaining a Security Descriptor (SD) file. That SD file contains the Access Control List (ACL) for each resource.

Two types of accounts are created and managed in Windows NT: machine accounts and user accounts. Both of these accounts are stored in the Security Account Manager database stored on the primary domain controller (PDC) and replicated to any backup domain controllers (BDC) on the system. Accounts are assigned an internally held system identification number (SID).

You create and manage accounts in the User Manager. Log on as an administrator so that you can fully access accounts for machines and different users. Other levels of users also have privileges, but what they can do is more limited. An account is specified by the machine and username, as in `<computername>\<username>`.

A *group* is an account that contains other accounts. Every computer contains a Users group to which all user accounts belong. There is also a Guest group that allows limited privileges to users who log in without a password (if you allow it).

The logon provides the definition of your group membership and other properties assigned to you. Groups can contain users as well as other groups that are given the same access rights to resources. Access privileges are cumulative when combining Share permissions or when combining Local permissions. When combining Share with Local, however, the most restrictive environment applies.

Local groups can be created to provide control over resource access. Windows NT also comes with some prebuilt global groups that are available systemwide. You can also define additional global groups. Users, groups, and domains offer a flexible system for managing resource access through security settings that you make either in the file system or on your desktop for various system objects.

Password Issues

Passwords enable you to log on to a particular user account. To log on successfully, you must know both the username and the exact password. The important thing to know about passwords is that they are *case sensitive*. Therefore, one of the most commonly encountered errors occurs when the Caps Lock key is pressed accidentally. A user can enter the correct password and still have his entry to the system denied because the password is entered in uppercase.

To protect passwords, Windows NT has an option that enables you to retire a password after a certain period of time. You can also set an option that requires Windows NT Workstation users to change the assigned passwords the first time they log on to the system. Users logging on after that time are required to change their passwords. Windows NT also allows a "no password" password for anonymous access, which provides limited access to system resources. This password might be used for a Web server running an FTP service, which enables a user to access a PUB folder, for example.

To change your users' password options, complete the following steps:

1. Select the User Manager from the Administrative Tools folder on the Programs submenu of the Start menu.

2. Choose the Policies | Account menu command. A dialog box appears.

3. In the Account Policy dialog box, select the options you desire, and then click OK.

The options of interest are listed here:

- **Minimum and maximum password age before a password expires.** In the days of old, when a user had to change his password, he would change it to its old value to make it easy to remember (for example, change Bob to Bob). To prevent this duplication, many network operating systems went with unique passwords, meaning that the user could not use the same password for a certain number of iterations (typically eight). Users then learned that when the change-password prompt came up, they could change Bob to Bob1 then Bob2 then Bob3, all the way up to Bob7 and back to Bob, on the same day. It took more work, but the result was the same. NT Workstation makes this much more difficult by allowing you to specify a minimum number of days the password must be used before it can be changed to something else. This setting requires a user to change his password when the maximum expires, but then will not let him change it again of his own accord until the minimum expires.

- **The minimum length of a password.** This length should be long enough to make it difficult to guess, but not so long that the user must write it on a Post-It note and stick the note to the top of the terminal, or you have defeated the whole purpose of security. Somewhere between 8 and 10 characters is sufficient for most installations.

- **Whether blank or no-character passwords are permitted.** Needless to say, allowing blank or no-character passwords does not do much for security. If security is of any concern, this option should definitely be disabled.

- **Whether a password list is maintained for an account and allows the user to cycle between passwords.** The password list ensures unique passwords for a number of iterations. It is highly recommended that this option be used to prevent expired passwords from becoming the new passwords.

- **How many failed attempts to log on with a username it takes to result in an Account Lockout.** Although a low number is good, know that it adds to administrative overhead. Every installation must find the perfect balance for that site.

If you use the Account Lockout feature, it is important to enter a Lockout Duration. After that duration, the account can be used again after a set of failed logons invalidates the account. If you are highly concerned about security, set this feature to require administrative action to unlock, and you will be able to keep track of most break-in attempts.

It is important not to have a very large number of workstation passwords expire at the same time in a domain. The changing of a large number of passwords at a time will require that the entire SAM be resynchronized across the domain—a time-consuming procedure.

By the way, the common method used to change your own password is to press Ctrl+Alt+Delete, and then click the Change Password button in the Windows NT Security dialog box. The use of the Ctrl+Alt+Delete keystroke to initiate a logon or password change is meant to prevent the posting of a spoofed Password Change dialog box and theft of a user account and associated password, because this is one of the most difficult key sequences to trap and spoof. An example of this cannot be shown in this book because pressing the key sequence also prevents screen captures from being created.

You should know for the exam that the Change Password button can be used to change not only the NT password, but other passwords (such as NetWare) as well.

Troubleshooting Profiles and System Policies

A user profile is created whenever a user logs on to Windows NT Workstation the first time. User profiles can be created that provide a specific configuration of the desktop, programs, accessories, printers, taskbar and Start menu, Help system bookmarks, and options in the Windows NT Explorer. This capability enables an administrator to provide a default profile that is used by a standard user in a domain.

Profiles offer a method for creating an environment based on the user account. To set this option or to check to see whether a problem with the environment can be corrected, select the user account in the User Manager utility, and then click the Profile button.

Check the User Environment Profile dialog box for the startup script that modifies the environment at logon. Scripts can be BAT (batch), CMD (OS/2), or EXE (program or executable) files. You can also create a new script and specify its location.

Profiles can be stored on the server and retrieved as a cached copy on a local machine when a user logs on. A stored local profile can be used when a problem occurs with a network connection or with a logon. To enable a user to have his profile and configuration travel with him regardless of which workstation he logs on to in the domain, you can create *roaming profiles.*

You can find user profile settings in the Windows NT Registry in the HKEY_CURRENT_USER key. To modify a user profile, complete the following steps:

1. Log on to the system with the username whose profile you want to modify.

2. Open the Registry Editor (REGEDT32.EXE).

3. Choose Options | Read Only Mode if you don't intend to make changes (optional).

4. Click on the HKEY_CURRENT_USER key to expand the settings, and then alter the setting you desire.

5. Close the Registry Editor.

Close the Registry Editor to have your new settings take effect. The actual information that the Registry reads for a user profile is contained in the NTUSER.DAT file of the User Profile folder. This file is cached on a local computer when the user profile is read.

If you want to modify your user profiles, you can find them stored in the c:\WINNT\Profiles folder. The default profile is in the Default User folder, with other user accounts contained in folders with the same name as the user account. Each user profile folder contains a directory of shortcuts or link (.LNK) files to desktop items and the NTUSER.DAT file. The following shortcuts are contained in these folders:

- Application Data. Any application data or settings are stored in this folder.

- Desktop. Shortcuts to files or folders are contained in the Desktop folder.

- Favorites. Any shortcuts to programs, folders, or favorite locations on the Web are stored in this folder.

- NetHood. This folder stores shortcuts to Network Neighborhood objects. This is a hidden folder.

- Personal. This folder contains program items.

- PrintHood. Any network printer connections and settings are stored in this folder. This is a hidden folder.

- Recent. The list of files that appear on the Documents menu are stored as shortcuts in this folder. This is a hidden folder.

- SendTo. This contains shortcuts to document items.

- Start Menu. Any items that appear on the Start menu are stored in this folder.

- Templates. Any template items stored to disk by a user are contained in this folder. This is a hidden folder.

A user profile cannot be opened and read in any text editor, because a .DAT file is a compiled binary file. It can be opened with REGEDT32.EXE or REGEDIT.EXE. The information contained in the <USERNAME>\NTUSER.DAT file is stored in the following subkeys of the HKEY_CURRENT_USER:

- AppEvents (sounds)

- Console (command prompt and installed applications)

- Control Panel (which Control Panels are accessible and their settings)

- `Environment` (system configuration)

- `Printers` (printer connections)

- `Software` (which software programs are available and their settings)

Working with System Policies

To enforce a set of rules on a computer, a network administrator can create a system policy that applies to a single user, a group of users, or all users in a domain. You create a specific policy with custom options in the System Policy Editor. This utility enables you to edit portions of the Windows NT Registry or edit system policy. Policies that you see in the System Policy Editor are contained in the `WINNT.ADM` and `COMMON.ADM` system policy template files. A template file is a set of stored Registry entries. You can modify a template file in the System Policy Editor, or you can create new template files.

> **NOTE** The System Policy Editor is not installed by default on many installations of NT Workstation. If it is not on your system, you can download it from the Microsoft Web site or get it from the Microsoft Windows NT Workstation Resource Kit.

System policy settings are stored in the Windows NT Registry in the `HKEY_CURRENT_USER` and `HKEY_LOCAL_MACHINE` keys. When you open the System Policy Editor in the Registry mode, you expose various keys in this area of the Registry.

System policy can restrict network logon or access, customize the desktop, or limit access to settings in the Control Panel. A system policy can be applied to a single user, a group of users, or all the users in a domain. Windows NT comes with two standard policies: Default Computer and Default User, both of which control options applied to all computers and users in a domain. You can create and enforce additional system policies.

With the System Policy Editor in Policy File mode, you create or modify system policy files (`.POL`) for the domain. Any modifications you make for a user, group, or computer in the system policy are written as entries into the NTCONFIG.POL file. For the changes to be enforced, you must save this file in the NETLOGON share on all domain controllers.

Accessing Shared Resources

Failure to access a share is one of the most common problems requiring resolution by an administrator. Files, shared folders (or simply shares), printer shares, and other shared resources require resource permissions. To create a share for an object, typically you right-click on the object and select the Sharing command. In many instances, the Sharing tab of the object appears and enables you to specify users, groups, and access privileges that are allowed.

The person who creates the resource "owns" the resource and has full privileges to it. The administrator also has full access to resources and can take ownership of it. When an administrator takes ownership of a resource, access to the resource from the original owner is denied. This is a safety mechanism to make it obvious that ownership has been removed and that the resource has been fully taken over.

If a user can't access a shared resource, he might not have the privileges required to do so. Try logging on under a different account to attempt to access that resource. If the resource has been accessed in the past under a particular user account, make sure that the resource is spelled correctly and that it has been located properly.

If there is a general problem accessing shared resources, you might want to open the Control Panel folder and check the Services Control Panel to see whether the various services responsible for validation services are running properly. These services are the following:

- ◆ NetLogon service
- ◆ Server service
- ◆ Workstation service

You should also check the Network Control Panel to ascertain whether the network bindings are correctly bound. These bindings are listed on the Bindings tab; you determine individual binding settings by selecting a binding and clicking the Properties button.

Inadvertent changes or even intentional changes to a user's group memberships in the User Manager or a change in system policy can also prevent access to resources that were previously permitted.

MODIFYING THE REGISTRY USING THE APPROPRIATE TOOL

Several problems can be directly related to Registry errors. The most common categories of problems are the following:

- ◆ Your computer won't boot properly or at all.

- ◆ Your computer looks or works differently than it once did.

- ◆ Your computer won't shut down correctly.

- ◆ You get the "Blue Screen of Death" resulting from a STOP error.

- ◆ A software or hardware component that operated correctly stops working without any physical changes being made to the files or to the device.

- ◆ Something stops working after you add new software or hardware, but the two are not known to be incompatible.

Windows NT 4.0 introduced the Registry database to this operating system, building on an early version in Windows NT 3.1 that stored OLE location information on object servers. The first complete Registry appeared in Windows 95, although the versions of both are different. The Registry is a database of settings and parameters. Among the features set by the Registry are the nature of the interface, operating system hardware and software settings, user preferences, and other settings. Before the Registry appeared in Windows NT and Windows 95, these settings appeared as sections and lines in various .INI files.

The Registry is hierarchical, and each branch is referred to as a hive. Individual subbranches are called keys, which are binary files. The top or first key of a hive is the primary key, and each key is composed of subkeys that take value entries. Most Registry entries are permanent, although some are session-dependent, transient, and never written to disk. An example of a transient key is the HKEY_LOCAL_MACHINE\Hardware as generated by automatic hardware detection by the Hardware Recognizer

(NTDETECT.COM for Intel computers). The Hardware key is an example of a session value. Another transient value is the information written as part of a logon for a session, including security tokens.

When you install software, either a program or a part of the operating system such as a device driver or service, new subkeys and value entries are written to the Registry. Uninstall these components to remove the information. Subkeys and value entries store information about hardware settings, driver files, environmental variables that need to be restored, as well as anything the application developer requires reference to.

Only members of the Administrators or Power Users group can access the Registry by default. You can assign other users rights to modify all or part of the Registry by hives, but you should think long and hard before doing so. The potential to compromise security or corrupt an installation is high. By default, any user can see the Registry files but cannot edit, delete, or copy Registry files without specific permission to do so.

Changing the Registry

You use the Registry Editor to view and modify the Windows NT Registry. Of the two versions of the Registry Editor, REGEDT32.EXE and REGEDIT.EXE, the former is more generally useful and offers more options.

These programs are not listed on the Start menu and are not found in the Administrative Tools folder, where you might expect to find them, to discourage their casual use. Their programs are located in the WINNT folder, and you can add them to your Start menu or run them from the Run prompt on the Start menu.

Whenever you change a setting in a Control Panel or alter your desktop, you are writing changes to the Registry associated with the user account profile with which you logged on. If you want to view and modify Registry information relating to services, resources, drivers, memory, display, or network components, you can use the Windows NT Diagnostic program (WINMSD). This utility is found in the <System Root>\System32 folder, or in the Administrative Tools folder on the Programs submenu of the Start menu. In WINMSD, you are limited to viewing only and are protected from making destructive changes.

When you alter a value in the Registry using the Registry Editor, the changes you can make are unlimited and can be hazardous to your computer's health. If you delete or modify a required key, you could cause your computer to malfunction. The only recovery method you can count on in that instance is to reinstall Windows NT or to use the Repair disk. Proceed with caution when working in the Registry, and consider wandering around with the files opened as read-only (use the Read Only menu command in the Registry Editor to achieve this) to begin with.

Registry Keys

The six root keys and their subtrees are shown here:

+ HKEY_CLASSES_ROOT. This subtree stores OLE, file, class, and other associations that enable a program to launch when a data file is opened. Although the HKEY_CLASSES_ROOT is displayed as a root key, it is actually a subkey of HKEY_LOCAL_MACHINE\Software.

+ HKEY_CURRENT_USER. All user settings, profiles, environment variables, interface settings, program groups, printer connections, application preferences, and network connections for the currently logged-in user are stored in the subkeys of this root key.

+ HKEY_LOCAL_MACHINE. This subkey contains information that identifies the computer on which the Registry is stored. Information in this key includes settings for hardware such as memory, disk drives, network adapters, and peripheral devices. Any software that supports hardware—device drivers, system services, system boot parameters, and other data—is contained in this subkey.

+ HKEY_USERS. All data on individual user profiles is contained in this subkey. Windows NT stores local profiles in the Registry, and the values are maintained in this subkey. Each time it is accessed, only two users are loaded: the current one (identified by the SID) and .Default. You can never see any other user without logging in as that user for purposes of security.

+ HKEY_CURRENT_CONFIG. The current configuration for software and any machine values are contained in this key. Among the settings stored in this root key are the display device setup and control values required to restore the configuration when the program launches or your computer starts up.

♦ HKEY_DYN_DATA. Transient or dynamic data is stored in this last key in the Windows Registry. This is there for compatibility with Windows 95 only, and because NT does not currently use Plug and Play, this key cannot be modified by the user.

When the system loads the Registry, most of the data is contained in the HKEY_LOCAL_MACHINE and HKEY_USERS keys. As an example of the kinds of changes you can make, individual settings you make in the Control Panels are written back to different keys in the Registry. You can modify those settings directly. When you make a mistake, however, and delete a key or value in the Registry Editor, you cannot use an Undo command to recover from this error.

When Windows NT boots your system, it uses the current copy of the Windows NT Registry. It is possible that during your last session you deleted a setting that is needed. If this is the case, the Last Known Good configuration can save you. It is the configuration as it existed the last time you were able to successfully log on. Being such, it enables you to recover from any critical deletion in the Registry that you made—provided that you recognize the error before logging on to your computer successfully again.

ADVANCED TECHNIQUES TO RESOLVE VARIOUS PROBLEMS

Windows NT comes with several diagnostic tools to help you optimize and tune the system and to correct error conditions. In many ways, the operating system is meant to be *self-tuning* and to require relatively few settings to be altered to make the computer run well. To track errors, Windows has a system of events that are recorded in log files. These events can be tracked and controlled, and they prove very useful in troubleshooting. This section delves into the Event logs in some detail.

To aid in solving network problems, Windows NT also offers you the Network Monitor. This utility enables you to examine and analyze network performance and utilization. Common network issues are also discussed in this section.

Working with the Event Logs and Event Viewer

Events are actions that occur on your system. The system itself generates events and records them in the System and Security log files. Applications record their events in the Application log. There are standard events that you see, and you can audit resources to add additional events. Many application developers use the event system to aid in analysis of their application. The Event Viewer enables you to view the Event logs and analyze them.

The Event logs are normally viewed by anyone who cares to see the information. You can also remote-view an Event log if you have the permission to do so on another machine. An administrator might want to restrict access to these logs from another machine so that the information is secure and can't be erased.

To restrict who can open the System or Application logs, you can set the following key

```
HKEY_LOCAL_MACHINE\System\CurrentControlSet\Services\EventLog\
<log_name>
```

so that the RestrictGuestAccess value of type REG_DWORD is set to 1. When the RestrictGuestAccess is set to 0 or doesn't exist, the default condition is for anyone to be able to access these two logs.

The log files are a first-in, first-out (FIFO) system. When the ultimate limit of a log file is reached, the oldest events are deleted to make room for new events. The default size is 512KB, and the oldest event stored is up to one week old. You can modify these settings from within the Event Viewer. To change the settings of the Event logs, complete the following steps:

1. Open the Event Viewer.

2. Choose the Log | Log Settings menu command.

3. Select the log type in the Change Settings for ... Log list box of the Event Log Settings dialog box.

4. Set the size of the log in the Maximum Log Size spinner.

5. Select one of the radio buttons in the Event Log Wrapping section to determine what happens to old events.

6. Close first the Event Log Settings dialog box and then the Event Viewer.

Many events occur so frequently that they can overwhelm the Event logs and make it difficult to determine what other error conditions or trends exist. By analyzing the Event logs, you can determine what event types are worth keeping and how often they should be noted.

Another useful option that the Event Viewer enables is the export of Event logs to data files. Several different output formats are offered to enable you to more easily analyze the data in the logs. You can export your log data to text file (.TXT), Event log file (.EVT), spreadsheet (.SYLK), and database data file (.DBF) formats, among others. Numerous third-party tools help analyze Windows NT Workstation log files.

The Event Viewer (like the Performance Monitor) is one of the Windows NT operating system's central diagnostic tools. Learning how to use this tool well will reward the administrator with a better-running workstation, less time spent tracking down errors, and a lower-stress existence.

If you want additional information about an event, double-click on that event to view the Event Detail dialog box. You will find the following information generated for an event:

- Date of event.
- Time of event.
- User account that generated the event. When applicable, this information is recorded in the Security log.
- Computer on which the event occurred.
- Event ID (the actual Event code).
- Source or component that recorded the error.
- Type of error: Success, Failure, Error, Information, or Warning.
- Category of event.
- Description of event.
- Data describing the event in hexadecimal form.

You can find many of the error messages in the documentation and resource kits for Windows NT Workstation. Microsoft also keeps a technical database that contains many of the reasons that error messages are generated. You can search the Knowledge Base on the Microsoft Web site or on the Microsoft network to obtain error information stored in the logs.

TechNet is a monthly CD-ROM subscription service that includes service packs, patches, and a collection of selected white papers.

Another database on CD-ROM is delivered to programmers as part of their subscription to the Microsoft Developer Network program. This database contains information about not only error conditions, but also internal error codes of interest to programmers. All levels of participation in MSDN result in your receiving this database.

The Event log is very flexible. You can turn event logging on and off for various resources by specifying the auditing properties for that resource. Many developers use the Event logs to record information specific to their applications.

The Event log is almost an embarrassment of riches. To help you find the particular event you need, the Event Viewer has a find and search function. By using the View menu, you can also filter the Event log derived from your own computer by any of the following:

+ Computer

+ Event date and time

+ Event ID

+ Event type

+ User

+ Source of the event

Network Diagnostics

Numerous network problems arise relating to both hardware and software configuration. Some of these problems require that you experiment with cabling and couplings; others can be solved with software that comes with Windows NT Workstation.

If you have a complex network installation, you might require diagnostic equipment to test your hardware. Often you can test individual components by rearranging their position in the network (swapping cables or boards) and isolating the offending piece of hardware.

Windows NT comes with a utility called the Network Monitor that can be very useful for diagnosing network activity. This Administrative Tools utility collects and filters network packets and can analyze network activity. This utility diagnoses only the computer it is running on.

The Network Monitor is a supplementary component of the Windows NT Workstation installation. To install this program, open the Network Control Panel's Service tab and click the Add button.

Network Monitor is both statistical and graphical. In the four panes of the Network Monitor, the current activity appears in real time. The parameters show you the level of activity your network is experiencing and how saturated your network bandwidth is. The Session Stats pane shows you which nodes are communicating and the number of frames (of the first 128 measured) sent and received from each.

The PING utility is also included in Windows NT Workstation. You can ping other computers on the network to see whether they are active, your own workstation with the specific address, the default gateway, and any computer on the Internet or your intranet. Use the PING command in a command prompt session without any other parameters to see an informational screen detailing its use.

Resource Conflicts

Many configuration errors are resource conflicts. These take the form of duplicate interrupt or I/O assignment or SCSI devices having duplicate assignments or improper assignments. You might see these problems when you first boot your system, or they might show up later when a device doesn't work properly.

Check the Event log to see what error events are listed. Also run the Windows diagnostic program WINMSD (in the Administrative Tools folder) to examine your resource settings. Errors in software can be rolled back using the Last Known Good configuration.

Using the Windows NT Diagnostics Program

The Windows NT Diagnostics program is the worthy successor to the MSD program found in Windows 3.1. This dialog box shows you information on many of the Registry items found in the HKEY_LOCAL_MACHINE subtree. Using WINMSD, you can obtain detailed information and reports on the state and configuration of your workstation. You cannot use this diagnostic tool to change any configuration settings, but you can use it to determine what conditions exist so that you can fix a problem.

This dialog box contains the following tabs:

* **Display.** Information on your video adapter, its firmware, and any adapter settings are found on this tab.

* **Drives.** A list of drives and volumes is contained in a hierarchical display. Drives include floppy disk drives, hard disk drives, CD-ROM, optical drives, and mapped drives through any network connections. If you double-click on a drive letter, the Drive Properties dialog box appears. This dialog box shows you cluster size, bytes per sector, the current status of the use of the disk, and the file system in use.

* **Environment.** Any environmental variables in use for a command prompt session appear on this tab.

* **Memory.** The installed memory, virtual memory, and usage of both is shown on this tab.

* **Network.** This tab shows any installed logons, transports (protocols and bindings), settings, and statistics.

* **Resources.** If you open this tab, the listing of device assignments appears. Shown here are the IRQ, port numbers, DMA channels, and UMB locations being used by each device. If you suspect a device conflict, this is the place to go to attempt to locate the suspect.

* **Services.** The information stored in the HKEY_LOCAL_MACHINE\System\CurrentControlSet\Services key is displayed on this tab. If you select a service and click the Devices button, the information stored in the HKEY_LOCAL_MACHINE\System\CurrentControlSet\Control key appears, along with the status of that control.

- **System.** The information stored in the HKEY_LOCAL_MACHINE\Hardware key shows the CPU type and information on other installed devices.

- **Version.** The information stored in the HKEY_LOCAL_MACHINE\Software \Microsoft\Windows\NT\CurrentVersion key is shown on this tab. You will find the operating system version, build number, service pack update, and name of the registered owner of the software.

WHAT IS IMPORTANT TO KNOW

The following bullets summarize the chapter and accentuate the key concepts to memorize for the exam:

- The `BOOT.INI` file provides the menu of operating systems shown on the boot menu.

- You hide a printer share by adding a dollar-sign character to the end of the share name, as in *sharename$*.

- A print job spooled to a printer is written as a temporary file to the `%systemroot%\System32\Spool\Printers` folder.

- Spooled print job files are deleted after the printer indicates that the job has been printed.

- The primary print spool problem encountered is a lack of available disk space.

- If you have a malfunctioning application, bring up the Task Manager and close down the process.

- If you need to end a 16-bit Windows or an MS-DOS application, you must close the entire session. When you close a 32-bit Windows application, only the particular process or thread needs to be closed.

Think of this as your personal study diary—your documentation of how you beat this exam.

The following section of Objective Review Notes is provided so you can personalize this book to maximum effect. This is your workbook, study sheet, notes section, whatever you want to call it. YOU will ultimately decide exactly what information you'll need, but there's no reason this information should be written down somewhere else. As the author has learned from his teaching experiences, there's absolutely no substitute for taking copious notes and using them *throughout* the study process.

There's a separate section—two to a page—for each subobjective covered in the book. Each subobjective section falls under the main exam objective category, just as you'd expect to find it. It is strongly suggested that you review each subobjective and immediately make note of your knowledge level; then return to the Objective Review Notes section repeatedly and document your progress. Your ultimate goal should be to be able to review only this section and know if you are ready for the exam.

OBJECTIVE REVIEW NOTES

Suggested use:

1. Read the objective. Refer to the part of the book where it's covered. Then ask yourself the following questions:

   - Do you already know this material? Then check 'Got it' and make a note of the date.

   - Do you need some brushing up on the objective area? Check "Review it" and make a note of the date. While you're at it, write down the page numbers you just checked, because you'll need to return to that section.

   - Is this material something you're largely unfamiliar with? Check the "Help!" box and write down the date. Now you can get to work.

2. You get the idea. Keep working through the material in this book and in the other study material you probably have. The better you understand the material, the quicker you can update and upgrade each objective notes section from "Help!" to "Review it" to "Got it."

3. Cross reference the materials YOU are using. Most people who take certification exams use more than one resource at a time. Write down the page numbers of where this material is covered in other books you're using, or which software program and file this material is covered on, or which video tape (and counter number) it's on, or whatever you need that works for you.

Planning

► Objective: Create unattended installation files.

☐ **Got it**   ☐ **Review it**   ☐ **Help!**
  Date:_____   *Date:_____*   *Date:_____*

Notes:

_____
_____
_____
_____
_____

Fast Track cross reference, see pages:

_____
_____

Other resources cross reference, see pages:

_____
_____
_____

► Objective: Plan strategies for sharing and securing resources.

☐ **Got it**   ☐ **Review it**   ☐ **Help!**
  Date:_____   *Date:_____*   *Date:_____*

Notes:

_____
_____
_____
_____
_____

Fast Track cross reference, see pages:

_____
_____

Other resources cross reference, see pages:

_____
_____
_____

OBJECTIVE REVIEW NOTES

►Objective: Choose the appropriate file systems to use in a given situation.

☐ Got it	☐ Review it	☐ Help!
Date:	*Date:*	*Date:*

Notes:

_____
_____
_____
_____
_____
_____
_____
_____

Fast Track cross reference, see pages:

_____
_____
_____
_____

Other resources cross reference, see pages:

_____
_____
_____
_____
_____
_____
_____

OBJECTIVE REVIEW NOTES

Installation and Configuration

► Objective: Install Windows NT Workstation on an Intel platform in a given situation.

☐ **Got it**　　☐ **Review it**　　☐ **Help!**
　Date:＿＿＿　　*Date:*＿＿＿＿　　*Date:*＿＿＿

Notes:

_____
_____
_____
_____
_____

Fast Track cross reference, see pages:

_____
_____

Other resources cross reference, see pages:

_____
_____
_____
_____

► Objective: Set up a dual-boot system in a given situation.

☐ **Got it**　　☐ **Review it**　　☐ **Help!**
　Date:＿＿＿　　*Date:*＿＿＿＿　　*Date:*＿＿＿

Notes:

_____
_____
_____
_____
_____
_____

Fast Track cross reference, see pages:

_____
_____

Other resources cross reference, see pages:

_____
_____
_____

OBJECTIVE REVIEW NOTES

▶ Objective: Remove Windows NT Workstation in a given situation.

☐ Got it	☐ Review it	☐ Help!
*Date:*_____	*Date:*_____	*Date:*_____

Notes:

_____
_____
_____
_____
_____

Fast Track cross reference, see pages:

_____
_____

Other resources cross reference, see pages:

_____
_____
_____
_____

▶ Objective: Install, configure, and remove hardware components for a given situation.

☐ Got it	☐ Review it	☐ Help!
*Date:*_____	*Date:*_____	*Date:*_____

Notes:

_____
_____
_____
_____
_____

Fast Track cross reference, see pages:

_____
_____

Other resources cross reference, see pages:

_____
_____
_____

OBJECTIVE REVIEW NOTES

▶ Objective: Use Control Panel applications to configure a Windows NT Workstation computer in a given situation.

☐ Got it	☐ Review it	☐ Help!
Date: _____	*Date:* _____	*Date:* _____

Notes:

_____
_____
_____
_____
_____
_____
_____

Fast Track cross reference, see pages:

_____
_____
_____
_____

Other resources cross reference, see pages:

_____
_____
_____
_____

OBJECTIVE REVIEW NOTES

OBJECTIVE REVIEW NOTES

► Objective: Upgrade to Windows NT Workstation 4.0 in a given situation.

☐ **Got it** / ☐ **Review it** / ☐ **Help!**
Date:_____ Date:_____ Date:_____

Notes:
_____
_____
_____
_____
_____
_____

Fast Track cross reference, see pages:
_____
_____

Other resources cross reference, see pages:
_____
_____
_____
_____

► Objective: Configure server-based installation for wide-scale deployment in a given situation.

☐ **Got it** / ☐ **Review it** / ☐ **Help!**
Date:_____ Date:_____ Date:_____

Notes:
_____
_____
_____
_____
_____

Fast Track cross reference, see pages:
_____
_____

Other resources cross reference, see pages:
_____
_____
_____

Managing Resources

▶ Objective: Create and manage local user accounts and local group accounts to meet given requirements.

☐ Got it	☐ Review it	☐ Help!
Date:____	Date:_____	Date:____

Notes:

_____
_____
_____
_____
_____

Fast Track cross reference, see pages:

_____

Other resources cross reference, see pages:

_____
_____
_____

▶ Objective: Set up and modify user profiles.

☐ Got it	☐ Review it	☐ Help!
Date:____	Date:_____	Date:____

Notes:

_____
_____
_____
_____
_____

Fast Track cross reference, see pages:

_____

Other resources cross reference, see pages:

_____
_____
_____

OBJECTIVE REVIEW NOTES

►Objective: Set up shared folders and permissions.

☐ **Got it**   ☐ **Review it**   ☐ Help!
Date:_____   *Date:_____*   *Date:_____*

Notes:

_____
_____
_____
_____
_____
_____

Fast Track cross reference, see pages:

_____
_____

Other resources cross reference, see pages:

_____
_____
_____
_____

►Objective: Set permissions on NTFS partitions, folders, and files.

☐ **Got it**   ☐ **Review it**   ☐ Help!
Date:_____   *Date:_____*   *Date:_____*

Notes:

_____
_____
_____
_____
_____
_____

Fast Track cross reference, see pages:

_____
_____

Other resources cross reference, see pages:

_____
_____
_____

OBJECTIVE REVIEW NOTES

► Objective: Install and configure printers in a given environment.

☐ Got it	☐ Review it	☐ Help!
*Date:*_____	*Date:*_____	*Date:*_____

Notes:
_____
_____
_____
_____
_____

Fast Track cross reference, see pages:
_____
_____

Other resources cross reference, see pages:
_____
_____
_____
_____

Connectivity

► Objective: Add and configure the network components of Windows NT Workstation.

☐ Got it	☐ Review it	☐ Help!
*Date:*_____	*Date:*_____	*Date:*_____

Notes:
_____
_____
_____
_____
_____

Fast Track cross reference, see pages:
_____
_____

Other resources cross reference, see pages:
_____
_____
_____

OBJECTIVE REVIEW NOTES

► Objective: Use various methods to access network resources.

☐ Got it   ☐ **Review it**   ☐ Help!
Date:_____   Date:_____   Date:_____

Notes:

_____
_____
_____
_____
_____

Fast Track cross reference, see pages:

_____
_____

Other resources cross reference, see pages:

_____
_____
_____
_____

► Objective: Implement Windows NT Workstation as a client in a NetWare environment.

☐ Got it   ☐ **Review it**   ☐ Help!
Date:_____   Date:_____   Date:_____

Notes:

_____
_____
_____
_____
_____

Fast Track cross reference, see pages:

_____
_____

Other resources cross reference, see pages:

_____
_____
_____

OBJECTIVE REVIEW NOTES

► Objective: Use various configurations to install Windows NT Workstation as a TCP/IP client.

☐ **Got it**
Date:_____

☐ **Review it**
Date:_____

☐ **Help!**
Date:_____

Notes:

_____
_____
_____
_____
_____

Fast Track cross reference, see pages:

_____
_____

Other resources cross reference, see pages:

_____
_____
_____

► Objective: Configure and install Dial-Up Networking in a given situation.

☐ **Got it**
Date:_____

☐ **Review it**
Date:_____

☐ **Help!**
Date:_____

Notes:

_____
_____
_____
_____
_____

Fast Track cross reference, see pages:

_____
_____

Other resources cross reference, see pages:

_____
_____
_____

OBJECTIVE REVIEW NOTES

Objective: Configure Microsoft Peer Web Services in a given situation.

☐ **Got it**   ☐ **Review it**   ☐ **Help!**
  Date: *Date:*   *Date:*

Notes:

_____
_____
_____
_____
_____

Fast Track cross reference, see pages:

_____
_____

Other resources cross reference, see pages:

_____
_____
_____
_____

Running Applications

Objective: Start applications on Intel and RISC platforms in various operating system environments.

☐ **Got it**   ☐ **Review it**   ☐ **Help!**
  Date: *Date:*   *Date:*

Notes:

_____
_____
_____
_____
_____

Fast Track cross reference, see pages:

_____
_____

Other resources cross reference, see pages:

_____
_____
_____

► Objective: Start applications at various priorities.

☐ **Got it**　　　☐ **Review it**　　　☐ **Help!**
*Date:*_____　*Date:*_____　*Date:*_____

Notes:

_____
_____
_____
_____
_____

Fast Track cross reference, see pages:

_____
_____

Other resources cross reference, see pages:

_____
_____
_____

Monitoring and Optimization

► Objective: Monitor system performance by using various tools.

☐ **Got it**　　　☐ **Review it**　　　☐ **Help!**
*Date:*_____　*Date:*_____　*Date:*_____

Notes:

_____
_____
_____
_____
_____
_____

Fast Track cross reference, see pages:

_____
_____

Other resources cross reference, see pages:

_____
_____
_____

OBJECTIVE REVIEW NOTES

Objective: Identify and resolve a given performance problem.

☐ **Got it**   ☐ **Review it**   ☐ **Help!**
*Date:*_____   *Date:*_____   *Date:*_____

Notes:

_____

_____

_____

_____

_____

_____

Fast Track cross reference, see pages:

_____

_____

Other resources cross reference, see pages:

_____

_____

_____

_____

Objective: Optimize system performance in various areas.

☐ **Got it**   ☐ **Review it**   ☐ **Help!**
*Date:*_____   *Date:*_____   *Date:*_____

Notes:

_____

_____

_____

_____

_____

_____

Fast Track cross reference, see pages:

_____

_____

Other resources cross reference, see pages:

_____

_____

_____

OBJECTIVE REVIEW NOTES

Troubleshooting

► Objective: Choose the appropriate course of action to take when the boot process fails.

☐ Got it	☐ Review it	☐ Help!
Date:_____	Date:_____	Date:_____

Notes:
_____
_____
_____
_____
_____

Fast Track cross reference, see pages:
_____
_____

Other resources cross reference, see pages:
_____
_____
_____

► Objective: Choose the appropriate course of action to take when a print job fails.

☐ Got it	☐ Review it	☐ Help!
Date:_____	Date:_____	Date:_____

Notes:
_____
_____
_____
_____
_____
_____

Fast Track cross reference, see pages:
_____
_____

Other resources cross reference, see pages:
_____
_____
_____

OBJECTIVE REVIEW NOTES

► Objective: Choose the appropriate course of action to take when the installation process fails.

☐ **Got it**   ☐ **Review it**   ☐ Help!
Date:_____   Date:_____   Date:_____

Notes:
_____
_____
_____
_____
_____
_____

Fast Track cross reference, see pages:
_____
_____

Other resources cross reference, see pages:
_____
_____
_____

► Objective: Choose the appropriate course of action to take when an application fails.

☐ **Got it**   ☐ **Review it**   ☐ Help!
Date:_____   Date:_____   Date:_____

Notes:
_____
_____
_____
_____
_____
_____

Fast Track cross reference, see pages:
_____
_____

Other resources cross reference, see pages:
_____
_____
_____

OBJECTIVE REVIEW NOTES

► Objective: Choose the appropriate course of action to take when a user cannot access a resource.

☐ Got it   ☐ Review it   ☐ Help!
  Date:_____   Date:_____   Date:_____

Notes:

_____
_____
_____
_____
_____

Fast Track cross reference, see pages:

_____
_____

Other resources cross reference, see pages:

_____
_____

► Objective: Modify the Registry using the appropriate tool in a given situation.

☐ Got it   ☐ Review it   ☐ Help!
  Date:_____   Date:_____   Date:_____

Notes:

_____
_____
_____
_____
_____

Fast Track cross reference, see pages:

_____
_____

Other resources cross reference, see pages:

_____
_____

OBJECTIVE REVIEW NOTES

► Objective: Implement advanced techniques to resolve various problems.

☐ Got it   ☐ Review it   ☐ Help!
   *Date:*_____   *Date:*_____   *Date:*_____

Notes:
_____
_____
_____
_____
_____
_____

Fast Track cross reference, see pages:
_____
_____

Other resources cross reference, see pages:
_____
_____
_____
_____

OBJECTIVE REVIEW NOTES

INSIDE EXAM 70-073

Part II of this book is designed to round out your exam preparation by providing you with the following chapters:

▶ "Fast Facts Review" is a digest of all "What Is Important to Know" sections from all Part I chapters. Use this chapter to review just before you take the exam: It's all here, in an easily reviewable format.

▶ "Insider's Spin on Exam 70-073" grounds you in the particulars for preparing mentally for this examination and for Microsoft testing in general.

▶ "Sample Test Questions" provides a full-length practice exam that tests you on the actual material covered in Part I. If you mastered the material there, you should be able to pass with flying colors here.

▶ "Hotlist of Exam-Critical Concepts" is your resource for cross-checking your tech terms. Although you're probably up to speed on most of this material already, double-check yourself anytime you run across an item you're not 100 percent certain about; it could make a difference at exam time.

▶ "Did You Know?" is the last-day-of-class bonus chapter: A brief touching-upon of peripheral information that's designed to be helpful and of interest to anyone using this technology to the point that he or she wishes to be certified in its mastery.

The exam is divided into seven objective categories:

- ▶ Planning
- ▶ Installation and Configuration
- ▶ Managing Resources
- ▶ Connectivity
- ▶ Running Applications
- ▶ Monitoring and Optimization
- ▶ Troubleshooting

CHAPTER 8

Fast Facts Review

WHAT TO STUDY

A review of the key topics discussed in the preceding seven chapters follows. After you are certain that you understand the principles given in those seven chapters, study these key points on the day of the exam before taking it.

Planning

The **command-line option for using an unattended installation script** is /U:filename. The **command-line option for using a uniqueness database file (UDF)** is /UDF:ID,filename. Not all options in the unattended installation file can be specified in the uniqueness database file. However, a single uniqueness database file can contain multiple IDs, so a single uniqueness database file can contain unique settings for multiple systems.

The **OEM structure allows complete control of the installation process**, but files in the OEM structure must conform to the 8.3 DOS file-naming convention. The $$RENAME.TXT file, on the other hand, controls the renaming of files in the OEM directory. Said OEM directory contains a file called CMDLINES.TXT that contains all the commands to run after the setup is complete, and OEM can include the SYSDIFF utility (used to automate the installation of applications as well as to configure Windows NT).

SYSDIFF must be run with the /snap mode to create a snapshot first. After the applications are installed and the configuration is changed, the /diff mode is used to create a differences file from the snapshot that can be applied to multiple computers (via the /apply mode).

SYSDIFF can create a completely different OEM directory from a differences file by using the /inf option, but the differences files can be applied only to systems that have the same installation directory as the system where the differences file was created.

Installation and Configuration

Minimum hardware requirements for Workstation 4.0 include a **486DX/33** processor, **12MB of RAM**, and at least **120MB of free disk space**. Setup is done through **WINNT or WINNT32**. WINNT is used for DOS and Windows. WINNT32 is for previous versions of Windows NT. Setup disks are created at installation or can be created at any later time by use of the /OX switch with WINNT or WINNT32. Any number of different versions of Windows NT can be installed on the same system for dual booting, as long as each version is installed in its own directory.

Windows NT Workstation **supports FAT and NTFS file systems** (OS/2's HPFS is no longer supported as of this release). FAT formatted file systems, though supporting no security at the file level, are required to boot RISC machines and Intel machines when dual booting to Windows 95 or DOS. NTFS, on the other hand, is a fault-tolerant file system with transaction tracking support that supports file-level security information and file-level compression.

Permissions and attributes between partitions can seem squirrelly unless you remember what is going on behind the scenes. If you **move a file between NTFS partitions**, the file is copied to the destination folder and then deleted from the first folder. In this instance, attributes of the target folder apply to the file. This is in contrast to **moving a file within the same NTFS partition**, in which the file keeps its same attributes. When you **copy a file**, regardless of whether it is to the same partition, the permissions of the target directory always are assigned to the new file. If you **copy or move a file from an NTFS partition to a FAT partition**, the permissions are always lost, yet the long filename (if there was one) is maintained.

Windows NT Workstation **supports membership in a workgroup or a domain.** It allows you to control access to resources at a share level, and all file permissions are enforced through the shares. As a rule, **the *most* restrictive permissions between the share and file permissions are used.**

If Workstation is installed on an Intel-based machine, a hidden, read-only file named **BOOT.INI is created in the root directory**. A sample of this file is shown here:

```
[boot loader]
timeout=30
default=multi(0)disk(0)rdisk(0)partition(1)\WINWKSTN
[operating systems]
multi(0)disk(0)rdisk(0)partition(1)\WINWKSTN="Windows NT Workstation
➥Version 4.00"
multi(0)disk(0)rdisk(0)partition(1)\WINWKSTN="Windows NT Workstation
➥Version 4.00 [VGA mode]" /basevideo /sos
multi(0)disk(0)rdisk(0)partition(1)\WINNT="Windows NT Server Version
➥4.00"
multi(0)disk(0)rdisk(0)partition(1)\WINNT="Windows NT Server Version
➥4.00 [VGA mode]" /basevideo /sos
C:\="Microsoft Windows"
```

This file is important because it represents the choices available at the boot menu. Note that there are **only two sections—[boot loader] and [operating systems]**. The first section defines the amount of time in seconds to wait before defaulting to an operating system and what the default operating system is. Changing the timeout parameter to 0 makes the boot menu no longer visible and always boots the default. Making the timeout parameter -1 forces the menu to not count down and always wait for the user to make a choice. The second part of boot.ini—the [operating systems] section—contains the valid choices installed on the workstation.

Managing Resources

Because NT Workstation can exist in a workgroup or a domain, users can log on locally, or they can log on and be authenticated by a server (NT or NetWare). It is important to remember that **when a user is logging on locally**, her **least restrictive level of access** (in other words, the level of permission for locally accessing an NTFS folder) **determines her level of resource access**. This is always the case unless there is a No Access permission anywhere in the mix, in which case **No Access prevails over all others** and the user has no access to the resource. If more than one user uses the workstation and you want to customize environments, a user account must be created for each user.

When logging onto a domain, the domain controller's NetLogon folder is checked for a **system policy (NTCONFIG.POL).** If the file is found, HKEY_CURRENT_USER and HKEY_LOCAL_MACHINE hives in the local Registry are overwritten with entries found there. For the entire domain, only one system policy needs to be created.

If logon scripts are used (their use is purely optional), they are replicated from \Winnt_Root\System32\Repl\Export\Scripts on the primary domain controller to the \Winnt_Root\System32\Repl\Import\Scripts on all backup domain controllers.

Users can join domains from their workstation if a computer account has been set up for them in the domain. They can do so by choosing Network in the Control Panel and then using the Domain Settings dialog box. When the user logs out and back in, he will attempt to connect to the new domain, because an individual user can be connected to only one domain at a time.

Only **members of the Administrators and Power Users groups can share folders** in Workstation. Other groups include Backup Operators, Guests, Replicator, and Users. Membership into groups and additional users are all added from the User Manager utility (not to be confused with User Manager for Domains, which exists only on NT Server).

When printers are shared, a priority setting can be applied in the printer's Properties dialog box that will determine which jobs are serviced by the print spooler first (higher priority jobs are always serviced first). Priority 1 is lowest, and 99 is highest.

Connectivity

Installing and configuring Windows NT Workstation 4.0 networking components can be done in a simple fashion. When you first install Workstation, the installation process examines your system for a network card; if one is located services are installed at that time. If you add a card later, or choose to change your services, you can easily make the change by following the steps of the wizard.

The Network Device Interface Specification (NDIS) is the specification that controls how network adapter card drivers need to be written. Windows NT 4.0 supports NDIS 3.0 and 4.0.

Although the names seem similar, don't make the common mistake of confusing the NetBEUI transport protocol with the NetBIOS API. NetBIOS and NetBEUI serve different functions in the networking components of Windows NT.

The **default protocol** for Windows NT Workstation 4.0 **is TCP/IP**. To configure it, you need an IP address, a subnet mask, and (optionally) a default gateway. An IP address is a unique, logical, 32-bit address used to identify a TCP/IP host. The subnet mask is a value used to determine whether a host is on the same or a different network. A default gateway is an optional setting in the TCP/IP configuration that identifies the router used to reach hosts not on the local network.

A DNS Server is used for name resolution identifying TCP/IP hosts on the Internet. WINS is used for IP resolution from NetBIOS names. The **IPCONFIG utility shows IP configuration information**, and IPCONFIG /ALL shows all of this information. The DHCP service allows IP configuration information to be dynamically leased to client computers. Static host and NetBIOS name resolution can be configured with the HOSTS and LMHOSTS files, respectively. They are located in \winnt_root\SYSTEM32\DRIVERS\ETC.

Share names, **computer names, and workgroup names are limited to 15 characters in length** and are often referenced by a UNC name, which takes the form of \\computername\sharename[\optional path].

Microsoft Client Service for NetWare (CSNW) must be installed with Windows NT Workstation **to access files or printers on a NetWare network**. Microsoft File and Print Services must be installed on an NT 4.0 Server if you need NetWare clients to access files and printers on an NT Server. This is a product available from Microsoft that is not included in the NT core product. NCP is the standard Novell protocol for file and print sharing. Large Internetwork Protocol (LIP) is used to negotiate and determine the largest frame size that can be used to communicate with a NetWare server.

If an NT Server is running Gateway Services for NetWare, a workstation client can access the NetWare network through the NT server. The two IPX/SPX (NetWare) frame types that CSNW detects are 802.2 and 802.3.

Windows NT **Workstation 4.0 supports two line protocols: SLIP and PPP**. SLIP is an industry standard that supports TCP/IP (and only TCP/IP) connections made over serial lines. Within Workstation, only the client functionality of SLIP is provided. PPP supports TCP/IP, NetBEUI, and IPX/SPX, as well as others. PPP also supports DHCP addressing, whereas SLIP does not. PPTP—the Point-to-Point Tunneling Protocol—is an extension of PPP that allows clients to connect to remote servers over the Internet and to create virtual private networks (VPNs).

A Windows NT Workstation is **limited to one RAS session at a time**. The three settings for it are Dial out only, Receive calls only, and Dial out and Receive calls, with Dial out only being the default. Dial-Up Networking supports most protocols. Authentication and encryption settings are set individually for each phonebook entry.

Whereas NT Server includes IIS (Internet Information Server), NT Workstation includes PWS (Peer Web Services). The functionality of the two products is much the same except that IIS allows for an unlimited number of connections, whereas PWS is limited to 10.

Running Applications

Sixteen-bit applications, whether for DOS or for 16-bit Windows, are all single threaded. **DOS applications are executed in individual NT Virtual Device Managers (NTVDMs) and do not share memory with each other** (they also do not support messaging).

Sixteen-bit Windows applications execute in a single Win16 NTVDM (though that can be changed to separate NTVDMs), share memory, and share a single message queue. They also employ cooperative multitasking, as opposed to 32-bit applications, which use preemptive multitasking (technically, applications in the Win16 NTVDM can be preemptively multitasked, though they must always share a common message queue).

The configuration files from the DOS world (CONFIG.SYS and AUTOEXEC.BAT) have been ported to Windows NT to configure 16-bit applications to run properly. They are now known as CONFIG.NT and AUTOEXEC.NT, and they serve the same purpose as they used to:

- CONFIG.NT loads system files.

- AUTOEXEC.NT primarily sets environment variables.

To cause 16-bit Windows applications to run in their own NTVDMs, use the Run command from the Start menu, or enter the START command from the command line.

Monitoring and Optimization

Various tools included with Windows NT Workstation can simplify monitoring and optimization tasks. These include the following:

- **Performance Monitor.** Shows statistics on just about everything, including memory usage statistics. **Physical disk counters are not visible in Performance Monitor, however, until you run DISKPERF.** Likewise, network performance monitors are not visible until the Network Monitor Agent is installed (this still does not give TCP/IP statistics unless SNMP has been installed as well).

- **Task Manager.** Shows running applications, CPU statistics, running processes, and memory utilization. **You can summon Task Manager by right-clicking on the taskbar or by pressing Ctrl+Alt+Del and choosing it from the menu.**

The secret to paging problems is **adding more RAM**. Short of that, you can move the paging file from the boot partition or create multiple paging files (one for each physical disk except the boot partition). Another solution for increasing optimization is to convert all FAT partitions to NTFS. You configure the paging file by choosing System from the Control Panel. Choose the Performance tab and click the Change button beside the Virtual Memory information. The properties sheet that appears allows you to adjust the size and location parameters of the paging file.

Troubleshooting

To hide a printer share, you add **a dollar-sign character to the end of the share name**, as in *sharename$*. This **prevents the printer from being visible** in the Connect To Printer dialog box (one of the steps in the Add a Printer Wizard). A user must know that this printer share exists and be able to enter both the correct name and the path to the printer share name to connect to that printer.

A print job spooled to a printer is written as a temporary file to the `%systemroot%\System32\Spool\Printers` folder. The file is deleted after the printer indicates that the job has been printed. The primary print spool problem encountered is a lack of available disk space. **When you print to the spooler, you create two files for each print job: the `.SPL` file, which is the actual print job spool file, and a shadow file, which is given a `.SHD` extension.** The shadow file contains additional information about the print job that is not part of the print job itself, such as owner and priority. If the computer crashes, `.SPL` and `.SHD` files remain in the default spool file until the service restarts and they are processed and printed.

If you have a malfunctioning application, bring up the Task Manager and close down the process. You can access the Task Manager by using either the mouse or the keyboard. If you need to end a 16-bit Windows or an MS-DOS application, you must close the entire session. When you close a 32-bit Windows application, only the process or thread needs to be closed.

To restrict who can open the System or Application logs, you can set the following Registry key

```
HKEY_LOCAL_MACHINE\System\CurrentControlSet\Services\EventLog\
<log_name>
```

so that the `RestrictGuestAccess` value of type `REG_DWORD` is set to 1. When the `RestrictGuestAccess` is set to 0 or doesn't exist, the default condition is for anyone to access these two logs.

In the Insider's Spin, you get the author's word on exam details specific to 70-073, as well as information you possibly didn't know—but could definitely benefit from—about what's behind Microsoft's exam preparation methodology. This chapter is designed to deepen your understanding of the entire Microsoft exam process. Use it as an extra edge; inside info brought to you by someone who teaches this material for a living.

CHAPTER 9

Insider's Spin on Exam 70-073

At A Glance: Exam Information

Exam Number:	70-73
Minutes:	90
Questions:	51
Passing Score:	705
Single-Answer Questions:	Yes
Multiple-Answer with Correct Number Given	Yes
Multiple-Answer Without Correct Number Given	No
Ranking Order	No
Choices of A–D	Yes
Choices of A–E	No
Objective Categories	7

The NT Workstation exam, as it is referred to, is officially known as *Implementing and Supporting Microsoft Windows NT Workstation 4.02.* It is computer administered and is intended to measure your ability to implement and administer the product in an enterprise environment. It builds on basic knowledge and assumes that the test candidate has a great deal of experience with the product. Fifty-one questions are asked, and a candidate has 90 minutes to answer them with a passing score of at least 705 (roughly translating to passing with 36 correct answers).

There are two types of multiple-choice questions on the exam: single-answer (always readily identified by a radio button) and multiple-answer with the correct number given. There are no multiple-answer questions without the correct number given. There are a limited number of click-on questions, for which you are given a property sheet and told to click on the item you would choose to meet the specifications given. The questions, overall, are very verbose, include a large number of exhibits, and have choices only from A to D.

Although Microsoft no longer releases specific exam information, at one time it was quoted that 85 percent of all who take a certification exam fail it. Common logic then indicates that only 15 out of every 100 people who think they know a product actually know it well enough to pass—a remarkably low number.

Quite often, administrators who *do* know a product very well and use it daily fail certification exams. Is it because they don't know the product as well as they think they do? Sometimes, but more often than not, it is because of other factors:

- They know the product from the real-world perspective, not from Microsoft's perspective.

- They are basing their answers on the product as it currently exists, not as it was when it was first released.

- They are not accustomed to so many questions in such a short time, or they are not accustomed to the electronic test engine.

- They don't use all the testing tools available to them.

The purpose of this chapter is to try to prepare you for the exam and help you overcome the four items listed previously. If you've been taking exams daily and don't think you need this information, skim the chapter and go on—odds are that you will still uncover some helpful tips. On the other hand, if you have not taken a lot of electronic exams or have been having difficulty passing them by as wide a margin as you should, read this chapter carefully.

GET INTO MICROSOFT'S MIND-SET

When taking the exams, remember that Microsoft is the party responsible for authoring the exam. Microsoft employees do not actually write the exams themselves, but instead *experts* in the field are hired on a contract basis for each exam to write questions. All questions, however, must adhere to certain standards and be approved by Microsoft before those questions make it into the actual exam. What that translates into is that Microsoft will never have anything in an exam that reflects negatively on the company. It will also use the exams for promotional marketing as much as possible.

Therefore, to successfully answer questions and pass the exams, you must put yourself into the Microsoft mind-set and see questions from its standpoint. Take the following question, for example:

1. Which network operating system is the easiest to administer in a small real-estate office:

    A. NetWare 3.12

    B. SCO UNIX

    C. Windows NT 4.0

    D. LAN Server

Although you could look at the question and make a sincere argument for at least three of the answers, only one answer will be correct on a Microsoft exam. Don't try to read too much between the lines, and don't think you're going to put a comment at the end of the exam arguing why another choice would be better. If you answer anything other than C in this instance, you might as well write this one off as a missed question.

UNDERSTAND THE TIME FRAME OF THE EXAM

When you take an exam, find out when it was written. In almost all cases, an exam goes live within three months of the final release of the product it is based on. Before the release of the exam, it goes through a beta process in which all the questions that can be on the exam are written. This exam version is then available for a short time (typically a week), during which scores on each question can be gathered. Questions that exam takers get right every time are weeded out as being too easy, and those that are too hard are weeded out as well.

When you take something like a major operating system (to remain nameless in this example) and create an exam for it, what you end up with is a time frame similar to the following:

1. The product goes into early beta.

2. A survey is done (mostly of beta testers) to find out which components of the product they spend the most time with and consider to be the most important. The findings are used to generate the objectives and the weighting for each objective.

3. The product goes to final beta.

4. Contract writers are hired to write questions on the product using the findings from the survey.

5. The product goes live.

6. The exam is beta-tested for one to two weeks, after which results on each question are evaluated, and the final question pool is chosen.

7. The service pack for the product is released.

8. The exam goes live.

9. Another service pack to fix problems from the first service pack and add additional functionality is released.

10. Yet another service pack comes out.

11. The option pack—incorporating service packs—is released.

12. You take the exam.

Now suppose that the product happens to be NT Server 4, and you receive a question such as this:

1. What is the maximum number of processors NT Server 4.0 can handle?

  A. 2

  B. 4

  C. 8

  D. 16

In the real world, the answer is C or D, depending on how you look at it: The end-user license agreement states that 8 is the limit, but NCR and other vendors make SMP servers capable of running NT on 16. When NT 4.0 first came out, however, the answer was B. Because the original exam questions were written to the final beta, the answer then was B and now is B. Microsoft has maintained the stance that it will test only on core products, not add-ons. Service packs, option packs, and the like are considered to be something other than core product.

With this in mind, you must *always* answer the questions as if you are addressing the product as it existed when you pulled it from the box, and before you did anything else with it—because that is exactly what the exam is written to. You must get into this mind-set and understand the time frame in which the exam was written, or you will fail exams consistently.

GET USED TO ANSWERING QUESTIONS QUICKLY

Every exam has a different number of questions, but most stick with the 90-minute time frame. If you run out of time, every question you have not answered is graded as a wrong answer. Therefore you should follow these suggestions:

1. Always answer every question, and never leave any unanswered. If you start running out of time, answer all the remaining questions with the same answer (C, D, or such) and then go back and start reading them. Using the law of averages, if you do run out of time, you should get 25 percent of the remaining answers correct.

2. Time yourself carefully. A clock runs at the upper-right corner of each screen. Mark all questions that require lots of reading or have exhibits, and come back to them after you've answered all the shorter questions.

3. Practice, practice, practice. Get accustomed to electronic questioning and answering questions in a short period of time. With so many exam simulators available, there is no reason for anyone to not run through one or two before plunking down $100 for the real thing. Some of the simulators are not worth the code they're written in, and others are so close in style to the actual exam that they prepare you very well. If money is an issue, and it should be, look for demos and freebies on Web sites. Try http://www.MeasureUp.com, which is an excellent example of a site where you can try some sample exams online.

If you do run out of time while working on a question, spend as much time as you want to on that last question. You will never time out with a question in front of you; you will be timed out only when you click Next to go from that question to the next one.

BECOME ACQUAINTED WITH ALL THE RESOURCES AVAILABLE TO YOU

An enormous amount of common sense is important here, and much of that common sense comes only as you get more used to the testing procedure. To summarize a typical sequence of events:

1. You study for an exam for a considerable period of time.

2. You call Sylvan Prometric (1-800-755-EXAM) and register for the exam.

3. You drive to the testing site, sit in your car, and cram on those last-minute details that won't stick with the others.

4. You walk into the center, sign your name, show two forms of ID, and walk back to a computer.

5. Someone enters your ID in the computer and leaves. You're left with the computer, two pieces of plain paper, and two No. 2 pencils.

6. You click the button on the screen to begin the exam, and the clock begins.

When you call Sylvan, be certain to ask how many questions are on the exam so that you know before you go in. Sylvan is allowed to release very little information (for example, what constitutes a passing score), but this is one of the few pieces of information Sylvan can pass along.

The exam begins the minute you click the button to start it. Before then, your time hasn't started. After you walk into the testing center and sit down, you're free (within reason) to do whatever you want to. Why not dump everything from your brain (including those last-minute facts you just crammed on in the parking lot) onto those two sheets of paper in front of you before starting the exam? The two sheets provide you with four sides—more than enough to scribble everything you've remembered—and you can refer to all this information later, during the 90 minutes.

When you click Start, the first question appears. Various types of questions are asked, including the type shown in Figure 9.1. (Because Microsoft does not readily make available—for obvious reasons—the capability to take screen shots of the exams, Figure 9.1 and all figures in this chapter are from a third-party emulator closely resembling the real thing.)

Look at the sample question briefly, but more importantly, look at the information on the screen. First, you can mark this question; doing so will allow you to see (at the end of the exam) any questions you thought were difficult and jump back to them. Never mark a question and go to the next one without choosing some answer. Even if you don't read the question at all and are saving it for later, mark it and answer C. That way, if you run out of time, you have a chance of getting the question right.

In the upper-right corner, you see the question number you are on. In the real exam, you also see the time remaining. Under the question are the possible answers. The radio buttons to the left of the answers indicate that there is only one correct answer.

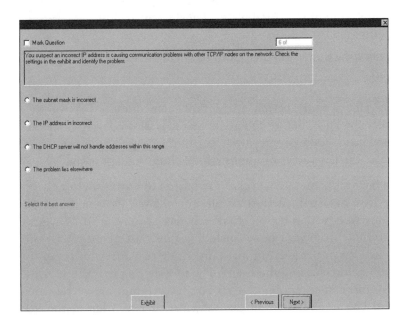

FIGURE 9.1
A sample test question.

Though not always true, many times when there are four possibilities, one is so far off the mark as to not even be plausible, one is too much of a give-me to be true, and you are left with two possibilities you must choose between. For example:

1. In NT Server 4.0, to view the Application log, what tool must you use?

    A. Application Viewer

    B. Event Viewer

    C. Event Observer

    D. Performance Monitor

In this case, choice A is the give-me of a nonexistent tool that fits the question too perfectly. Choice D is the blow-off answer so far away from what's possible as to not be considered. That leaves choices B and C.

Even if you know nothing about NT Server, a clue that B and C are legitimate possibilities is the closeness in their wording. Anytime you see two possibilities worded so closely, assume they are the ones to focus on.

The buttons at the bottom of the screen allow you to move to the next question or a previous question. The latter option is important, because if you come across a question whose wording provides the answer to a question you were asked before, always use the previous button to go back and change or check your first answer. Never walk away from a sure thing.

If an exhibit is associated with the question, the command button for it will be displayed as well. The problem with exhibits is that they either layer on top of the question or can be tiled in such a way that you can't see either one. Whenever you have an exhibit, read the question carefully, open the exhibit, memorize what is there (or scribble information about it on your paper), close the exhibit, and answer the question.

Figure 9.2 shows an example of a question with more than one correct answer—a fact obvious by the existence of check boxes instead of radio buttons to the left of the choices.

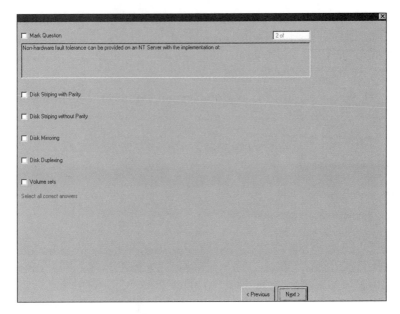

FIGURE 9.2
Another sample test question.

There are two types of these questions: For one you are told how many answers are correct (choose 2, choose 3, and so on), and for the other you are not. In the example shown, you are told to choose all correct answers, and you do not know whether that is two, three, or four. The only thing you do know is that the number of correct answers is not one and not five—Microsoft does not use check boxes if radio boxes work, and it never has an all-of-the-above type of question.

Most multiple-answer questions offer four possibilities, meaning that you must choose two or three, but those with five possibilities (as in Figure 9.2) are not uncommon. With multiple-answer questions, read the question as carefully as possible, and begin eliminating choices. For example, the question in Figure 9.2 specifically says *non-hardware* and one of the choices is duplexing. Duplexing requires a hardware enhancement over mirroring, so choice D is not correct. You are now left with four possibilities, and you must rely on your knowledge to choose the right ones.

The biggest problem with multiple answers is that there is no such thing as partial credit. If you are supposed to choose four items but you choose only three, the question is still counted wrong. If you should choose two and you pick one right answer and one wrong answer, you miss the whole question. Spend much more time with multiple-answer questions than single-answer questions, and always come back if time allows after the exam and reread them carefully.

After you complete the exam, if there is time remaining, you come to an Item Review section similar to that shown in Figure 9.3.

From here you can see the questions you marked and jump back to them. If you've already chosen an answer on that screen, it remains chosen until you choose something else (the question also remains marked until you unmark it). The command buttons at the bottom of the question will now include an Item Review choice to let you jump back to the Item Review screen without going through additional questions.

Use the capability to mark and jump as much as you possibly can. All lengthy questions should be marked and returned to in this manner. Also note all answers that are incomplete. You can ill afford to not answer any question, so be certain to go back and answer them all before choosing to finish the exam (or running out of time).

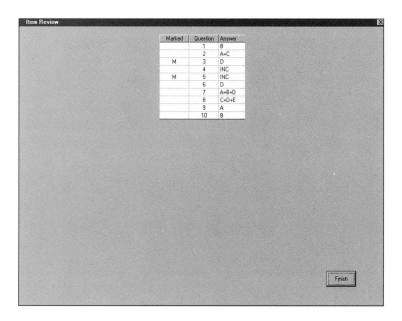

FIGURE 9.3
The Item Review at the completion of the exam.

After you click Finish, grading is done, and the Examination Score Report appears. The Score Report shown in Figure 9.4 is a bit misleading. Typically, you're shown only the bar graphs and a message indicating whether you've passed or failed. The Section Analysis does not appear on the screen, but only on the printed documentation you walk out of the testing center with. The pass/fail score is based on the beta of the exam and on statistics gathered from the performance of those who took part in it.

If you fail an exam—and everyone will occasionally—*never* be lulled into a false sense of confidence by the Section Analysis. If it says you scored 100 percent in a particular section, you should still study that section before retaking the exam. Too many test-takers study only the sections they did poorly on. That 100 percent in Monitoring and Optimization could be the result of the first question pool containing only one question, which you had a 25 percent chance of guessing correctly. What happens the next time, when there are three questions in the random pool from that objective category and you don't know the answers? You're handicapping yourself right off the bat.

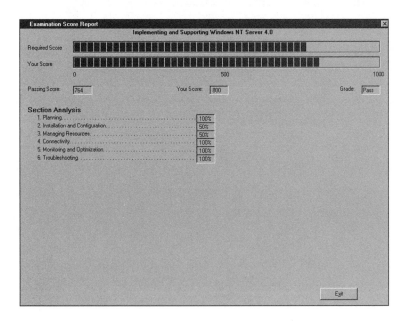

FIGURE 9.4
The Examination Score Report.

A good rule of thumb if you do fail an exam is to rush back to your car as quickly as you can and write down all the questions you can remember. Have your study materials in the vehicle with you, and look up the answers then and there. If you wait until later, you'll forget many of the questions.

The new policy from Microsoft allows you to retake an exam you fail once without any waiting period (other than registering for it and such). If you fail it again, however, you must wait 14 days before you can take it a third time (and 14 days from that point for the fourth try, and so on). This is to prevent people from actually memorizing the exam. Do your best to never fall into this category. If you fail an exam once, start all over again and study anew before trying it the second time. Make the second attempt within a week of the first, however, so that topics are fresh in your mind.

WHERE THE QUESTIONS COME FROM

Knowing where the questions come from can be as instrumental as anything in knowing how to prepare for the exam—the more you know about it, the better your odds of passing. Earlier, this text pointed out the time frame used to create the exam and that contract writers are hired for the exam. The contract writers are given a sizable document detailing how questions must be written. If you really want to pursue the topic with more fervor, contact Microsoft and inquire about a contract writing position. A few tidbits that can be gleaned from multiple-choice authoring, however, include the following:

1. No question should have an All of the Above answer. When such a choice is available, it is almost always the correct answer, and thus it is not a fair representation of a valid multiple-choice question.

2. For the same reason, there should never be a None of the Above answer.

3. Scenarios should be used when they increase the value of the question.

4. All subjective words (best, most, and so on) should be omitted from questions.

5. Although there can be only one correct answer for the question, all other possibilities should appear plausible and avoid all rationale or explanations.

6. Single answers must be mutually exclusive (no A+C, B+C, and so on).

7. Negative words should be avoided (not, cannot, and so on).

DIFFERENT FLAVORS OF QUESTIONS

At one time, all questions were either single-answer or multiple-answer. There is a push today to go more toward *ranking* questions and performance-based questions. Older exams still have only the first two question types, whereas newer ones offer the latter two types.

Ranking questions provide you with a scenario, a list of required objectives, a list of optional objectives, and a proposed solution, and then ask you to rank how well the solution meets the objectives. Here's a rudimentary example:

1. Evan is a teenager who just got his driver's license. He wants to buy a fast car and ask Betty Lou to the movies on Friday.

Required objectives:	Buy a fast car Ask Betty Lou to movies
Optional objectives:	Earn money for movies Earn money for car
Solution:	Take part-time job at the Qwik-E-Mart and buy classic '67 Cougar

Rank the solution in terms of the objectives:

A. The solution meets both required and optional objectives.

B. The solution meets both required objectives but only the first optional objective.

C. The solution meets both required objectives but only the second optional objective.

D. The solution does not meet the required objectives.

In this over-simplified example, the answer is D—the solution does not include asking Betty Lou to the movies so it does not meet the required objectives. With ranking questions, it is often the case that the required objectives are needed in all but the last answer, so read the question backward, so to speak, and see whether the required objectives are being met. If they are not, you can answer the question quickly without reading any further and can go on to the next question.

Performance-based questions have been incorporated in electronic testing for a long time, not just with Microsoft testing. If I really want to test and see how well you know a product before hiring you, the best way to do so is to turn you loose with the product and tell you to do something. If you can do what I ask, I'll hire you; if you can't, I won't.

Taking that scenario into the testing center becomes difficult for several reasons: First and foremost, you can't be allowed unrestricted access to the product within the confines of something (a shell) grading your actions. Second, the stability of the operations on most testing centers' antiquated machines is questionable at best. Third, the amount of time allotted cannot exceed a reasonable amount or you will become exhausted, and the testing center will not be able to move as many people through each day.

The solution to many of these problems is to keep the number of performance-based questions to a minimum and to have you work with an emulator of some type. The emulator can come on the screen when you click the button and can bring up something that looks like what the configuration information in the real product would be, without the time and overhead involved in bringing up the real product.

How do you prepare for performance-based questions? Know your product—plain and simple. Focus on the administrative side of it—how to add new users, sites, servers, directories, and so on—and you will have no difficulties. If you are very good at guessing multiple-choice answers but you really don't know the product at all, these questions will ferret out your lack of knowledge. On the other hand, if you know the product extremely well but just aren't good at multiple-choice guessing, you'll find these questions a godsend.

Regardless of your familiarity (or lack thereof) with the product, be very careful with all the performance-based questions. Although the emulator can load much quicker than the actual product in question, it is still very time-consuming, and the amount of time required to answer each question is far from small. These questions take *a lot* of time, and you need to budget for them accordingly.

IN THE FUTURE

The study of test delivery and grading is known as psychometrics, and a good many people are employed in this profession. Microsoft uses many of them to help with the design and implementation of its exams. It should come as no surprise (if you have any experience with other certifications, such as Novell's) that the next big push will be to *adaptive* testing.

Under adaptive testing, the amount of time for each exam can be reduced from 90 minutes to somewhere near 30, and the number of questions can drop from somewhere between 50 and 70, down to 15 or so. This benefits you greatly and allows more students to be tested each day at training centers.

The premise behind adaptive testing is fairly simple: The first question you get is pulled from a pool totally at random. Beyond that first question, every other question presented to you is in some way related to how well you answered the preceding question.

For example, suppose I want to give you a general exam on astronomy. The first question that comes up asks you how many planets are in our solar system. You answer correctly (nine). I now ask you to name the third planet from the sun, and you answer it correctly also (Earth). I can now assume that you know your planets very well, and the next question is about quasars. We do this for 15 questions, and if you answer them all correctly, I assume that you really know astronomy and pass you.

If, on the other hand, you answer Mars to the second question, the next question will be about planets again—giving you a chance to redeem yourself. If you miss that one, I'll probably ask the most difficult question known to mankind about planets to see whether you can get it right. If you can't, you don't know planets, and thus you don't know astronomy, and you'll fail. In some versions of adaptive testing, you bomb out right then because there is no chance of redemption; in others, you are just given bogus questions for the remainder of the exam to make you feel as though you're getting your money's worth, even though you are going to fail anyway.

Again, the process differs according to the style/vendor involved, but with most adaptive tests, if you answer the 15 questions and have not passed, but yet are very close to doing so, you can be asked additional questions. The additional questions give you the opportunity to redeem yourself and achieve a passing score.

The key to adaptive testing, besides each question's relationship to the one preceding it, is that every question has a point value associated with it. The first questions presented are assumed to be of medium value. If you miss a question on a particular topic, the next one asked will be more difficult, and of a higher point value to allow the chance for redemption. If you answer the first question correctly the next one will be of lesser value and lesser difficulty.

There is no Item Review in adaptive testing, and there is no going back to previous questions. After you answer a question, you are done with it, and you can draw a fair conclusion on how you did by whether the next question is on a similar topic.

Performance-based testing is in its infancy stages now at Microsoft, and it should be rolled out within the year. Again, the best preparation here is to know your topic and spend time with each question, making certain you fully understand what is being asked before answering. With performance-based testing, you are given a task to do in an emulator of the product you are testing on. Your performance is graded to see whether you completed the task in the time and manner in which an administrator should.

This is an exam preparation book. It's the belief of the author and publisher that it's difficult to get too much practice with sample exam questions. There are other study materials available—books and software—that enable you to practice extensively, and we recommend that you give strong consideration to using these in some form.*

What follows in this chapter is a practice test designed to reflect the questions you'd likely be challenged with on an actual Microsoft exam. These questions tie in directly to the material covered in this book. Take note that when this exam goes to an adaptive format, the number of questions, passing score, and minutes necessary to take this exam will vary.

Please see the end matter of this book for more information on New Riders TestPrep books and New Riders Top Score exam preparation software, among other New Riders certification study resources.

CHAPTER 10

Sample Test Questions

QUESTIONS

Please note: When this exam goes to an adaptive format, the number of questions, passing score, and minutes given to take the exam will vary. This sample test has 51 questions, just like the actual exam, and covers each of the seven objective categories.

1. *Kristin is running Windows NT Workstation on her machine at a small law firm that employs workgroups. After months of trying, she finally convinced her supervisors that she needed an HP 4000se laser printer. Now that it's properly installed and configured, she wants to share it, but only with select users. How can she hide the printer from most users so that they won't know it is there, yet make it available to those with whom she wants to share it?*

   A. Select the Hidden option on the Properties tab.

   B. Not install File Sharing.

   C. End the share name with a $.

   D. Create a global group that includes only the selected users.

2. *Evan is concerned because print jobs he sends to his printer are not coming out. He is not getting errors on his workstation to indicate that there is any problem with the configuration, but he is not getting the printed document from his printer. He questions whether the documents are printing to another printer or staying in the spool. To troubleshoot the problem, you should look to see whether there are spool jobs in which of the following folders?*

   A. `%systemroot%\System32\`

   B. `%systemroot%\System32\Spool\`

   C. `%systemroot%\System32\Spool\Printers`

   D. `%systemroot%\System32\Spool\Printers\Temp`

3. *Spencer complains that he cannot share folders with other users in his workgroup. Spencer is running Windows NT 4 and suspects that the problem might lie in his group memberships. What groups are allowed to share folders in NT Workstation?*

   A. Administrators

   B. Backup Operators

   C. Replicators

   D. Power Users

4. *Karen is attempting to troubleshoot a problem that's causing her applications to behave erratically. To that end, she has brought up the utility shown in Figure 10.1. What utility is she using?*

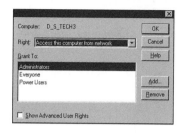

FIGURE 10.1
The utility Karen is using to troubleshoot application problems.

A. Performance Monitor

B. Task Manager

C. Disk Administrator

D. User Manager

5. *In reference to question number 4, what utility should Karen be using?*

A. Performance Monitor

B. Task Manager

C. Disk Administrator

D. User Manager

6. *Allan is installing Windows NT Workstation 4.0 on an Intel-based machine in an existing domain. What networking protocol(s) is/are installed by default?*

A. IPX/SPX

B. NetBEUI

C. TCP/IP

D. NetBIOS

7. *The head of the finance department, Madonna, comes to you with news that the company has just purchased a small consulting company in a nearby town. The company has seven Windows NT workstations that are currently functioning in a workgroup environment. What type of server can be added at the site to provide centralized user authentication? (Choose all that apply.)*

   A. NetWare
   B. Windows 95
   C. Windows NT Workstation
   D. Windows NT Server

8. *Which of the following utilities is used to automate the installation of applications and to configure Windows NT?*

   A. Performance Monitor
   B. Task Manager
   C. SYSDIFF
   D. Setupmgr

9. *In the unattended setup automation utility, which parameter creates a snapshot?*

   A. /snap
   B. /diff
   C. /apply
   D. /ox

10. *Lorraine would like to know whether her machine is capable of running Windows NT Workstation. To find the answer, she should look for the current:*

   A. HAL
   B. HCL
   C. BOOT.INI
   D. LAH

11. *Which of the protocols shown in Figure 10.2 is considered non-routable?*

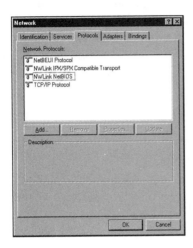

FIGURE 10.2
The currently installed protocols.

   A. NetBEUI
   B. NWLink IPX/SPX-Compatible Transport
   C. NWLink NetBIOS
   D. TCP/IP

12. *Your company has an employee named Jerry who likes to tinker with the system until it no longer works. Therefore, you must implement a system policy. Which of the following names is typically given to the system policy?*

   A. CONFIG.POL
   B. NTCONFIG.POL
   C. USER.DAT
   D. NTUSER.DAT

13. *Suppose that logon scripts must also be used on a domain network to curb rogue users like Jerry who like to tinker. Where should the logon scripts be placed (assume that replication occurs naturally)?*

   A. On the PDC
   B. On the BDC
   C. On the local machine
   D. In HKEY_CURRENT_USER

14. *Jennifer, the system administrator for ABC Solutions, would like to restrict access on one particular file containing performance reviews. When she attempts to highlight the file and change the permissions, however, she sees only the rights and information shown in Figure 10.3. Why is Jennifer unable to change the permissions on this file?*

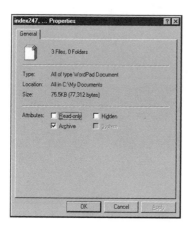

FIGURE 10.3
The properties on a selected file.

A. She does not have appropriate permissions.

B. The file is currently open.

C. The partition is FAT.

D. The owner has locked the account.

15. *Tony Co. is running a small network that consists of only Windows 95 and Windows NT Workstation clients on a Windows NT Server network. The Workstation bindings match those shown in Figure 10.4. Given this scenario, which protocol should be bound first?*

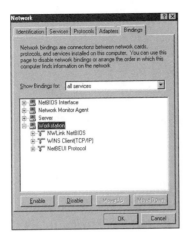

FIGURE 10.4
The binding order on Tony Co.'s Windows NT workstations.

    A. TCP/IP
    B. NetBEUI
    C. NWLink NetBIOS
    D. Doesn't matter

16. *The answer to most problems related to paging files is to:*
    A. Increase the speed of the processor.
    B. Add more RAM.
    C. Decrease the load.
    D. Install more hard drives.

17. *The paging file is configured from which Control Panel utility?*
    A. Service
    B. Network
    C. Memory
    D. System

18. *Windows NT Workstation can be installed into partitions currently (un)formatted as which of the following?*
    A. NTFS
    B. FAT
    C. HPFS
    D. CDFS
    E. Unformatted

19. *Which of the following partitions contains the system files?*
    A. boot
    B. system
    C. FAT
    D. NTFS

20. *Which of the following partitions contains the boot files?*
    A. boot
    B. system
    C. FAT
    D. NTFS

21. *Which of these utilities is used to format a partition in Windows NT Workstation?*
    A. User Manager
    B. User Manager for Domains
    C. Disk Administrator
    D. Format Manager

22. *Edna calls and is as mad as you have ever seen her. She is attempting to gather statistical information about her physical disk usage by using Performance Monitor. However, the graph she is getting, shown in Figure 10.5, shows a lack of activity. What is causing this lack of activity?*
    A. Her disk is experiencing no activity.
    B. Performance Monitor is not the appropriate tool to use.
    C. The physical disk counters are not turned on.
    D. She has selected the wrong hard drive.

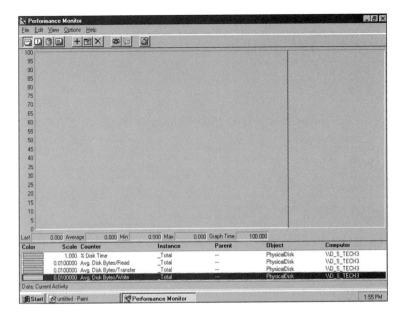

FIGURE 10.5
Edna's physical disk statistics in Performance Monitor.

23. *The Task Manager can be used to show running applications, memory usage, and so on. How do you bring it up?*

   A. Right-click on the taskbar.

   B. Press Ctrl+Alt+Del and choose it from the menu.

   C. Select it from the Administrative Tools folder on the Program submenu of the Start menu.

   D. Right-click on the desktop and choose Task Manager.

24. *Just when you are starting to enjoy work, Edna calls again. This time she is furious that Performance Monitor is not showing her the TCP/IP statistics even though she knows she has selected the appropriate counters. What is the problem this time?*

   A. She is probably not using TCP/IP; thus there is no activity.

   B. Performance Monitor is not the appropriate tool to use.

   C. The TCP/IP counters are not turned on by default.

   D. She has selected the wrong protocol.

25. *Windows NT supports which two of the following line protocols?*
    A. TCP/IP
    B. IPX/SPX
    C. PPP
    D. SLIP

26. *How many concurrent RAS sessions is Windows NT Workstation limited to?*
    A. 0
    B. 1
    C. 128
    D. 256

27. *How many concurrent RAS sessions is Windows NT Server limited to?*
    A. 0
    B. 1
    C. 128
    D. 256

28. *Mitch loves to play computer games during his lunch hour. He is holding back on upgrading to Windows NT Workstation— although the rest of the department has already done so—because he is afraid he will lose this capability. Given that the true work Mitch does is very minimal and game playing is his biggest concern, which operating system should he be using?*
    A. Windows for Workgroups
    B. Windows 95
    C. Windows NT Workstation
    D. Windows NT Server

29. *Which of the following statements are true of 16-bit Windows applications?*
    A. They employ preemptive multitasking.
    B. They run in their own message queues.
    C. They share a single message queue.
    D. They employ cooperative multitasking.

30. *What is the effect of the command-line command shown in*
    Figure 10.6?

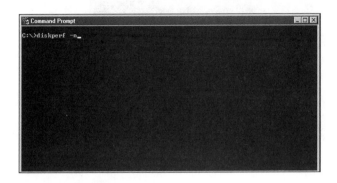

FIGURE 10.6
A command-line command.

A. Task Manager is started.
B. Physical disk statistics are no longer available in Performance
   Monitor.
C. FAT partitions are converted to NTFS.
D. Disk compression is activated.

31. *Two configuration files from the DOS world have been ported to*
    Windows NT to configure 16-bit applications to run properly.
    They are now known as:
    A. CONFIG.SYS and AUTOEXEC.BAT
    B. USER.DAT and SYSTEM.DAT
    C. CONFIG.NT and AUTOEXEC.NT
    D. CONFIG.NT and AUTOEXEC.BAT

32. Which system file is shown in Figure 10.7?

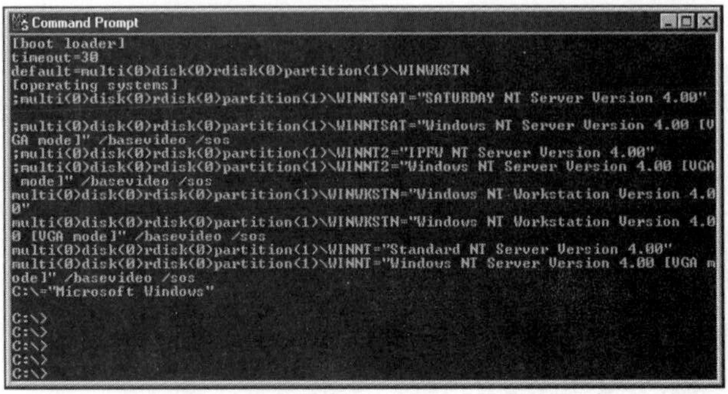

FIGURE 10.7
One of the system files.

    A. CONFIG.NT

    B. AUTOEXEC.NT

    C. USER.DAT

    D. BOOT.INI

33. In the startup file, the TIMEOUT= number should be changed to what to prevent the menu from appearing?

    A. -1

    B. 0

    C. 1

    D. ;

34. The startup file can be safely edited without using a command-prompt editor through which System utility tab?

    A. BOOT

    B. STARTUP/SHUTDOWN

    C. ENVIRONMENT

    D. GENERAL

    E. PERFORMANCE

35. *Landon is a temporary employee on a long-term assignment. Although he will be working for the company for quite some time, he must work at a different machine each day, depending upon whose regularly scheduled day off it is. To best accommodate these circumstances, Landon should be set up with a:*

    A. User profile

    B. Mandatory profile

    C. Roaming profile

    D. System profile

36. *To create a mandatory profile for a user, you use which of the following file extensions?*

    A. .DAT

    B. .PRO

    C. .NT

    D. .MAN

37. *Which of the following utilities is used to examine the System log?*

    A. Performance Monitor

    B. Event Viewer

    C. System Manager

    D. Task Manager

38. *McKenzie is trying to determine what type of machine she should purchase to run Windows NT Workstation at home. She has already decided to purchase a Pentium with a 5GB IDE drive. How much RAM is considered the minimum?*

    A. 4MB

    B. 8MB

    C. 12MB

    D. 16MB

39. *The share name is traditionally limited to how many characters?*

    A. 8.3

    B. 10

    C. 15

    D. 256

40. *The UNC path takes the form of:*

   A. `\\computername\sharename [\optional path]`
   B. `\\sharename\computername [\optional path]`
   C. `\\sharename [\optional path]`
   D. `\\computername [\optional path]`

41. *What would be the UNC path for a file named* SHANNON.DAT *in a directory named* WILLIAM *in a share named* JAN *on a server named* BOB?

   A. `\\JAN\BOB\WILLIAM\SHANNON.DAT`
   B. `\\SHANNON.DAT\WILLIAM\JAN\BOB`
   C. `\\BOB\JAN\WILLIAM\SHANNON.DAT`
   D. `//SHANNON.DAT/WILLIAM/JAN/BOB`

42. *For Jeff's workstation to join a domain, he must have network connectivity to which of the following?*

   A. A member server
   B. The backup domain controller
   C. The primary domain controller
   D. Another workstation

43. *A Windows NT workstation can access NetWare servers via a Windows NT server if the NT server is running which of the following?*

   A. Gateway (and Client) Services for NetWare
   B. Microsoft Client Services for NetWare Networks
   C. Microsoft File and Print Services for NetWare
   D. IPX/SPX

44. *CSNW is installed from which Control Panel applet?*

   A. Network
   B. System
   C. Services
   D. User Manager for Domains

45. *Which of the following is the command-line option for using an unattended installation script?*

   A. `/ox`
   B. `/U:filename`
   C. `/UDB:filename`
   D. `/S:filename`

46. Figure 10.8 shows which of the following utilities?

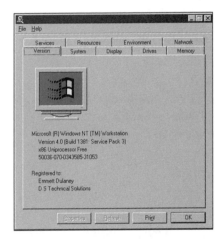

FIGURE 10.8
One of the system utilities.

A. Windows NT Diagnostics
B. User Manager
C. Disk Manager
D. Event Viewer

47. Tracy calls with a question about some errors that are appearing in the System log. Figure 10.9 shows the errors in the Event Viewer. Of the four events shown, which one most likely caused the other three?

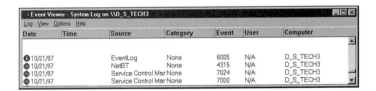

FIGURE 10.9
The System log in Event Viewer.

A. Event 6005
B. Event 4315
C. Event 7024
D. Event 7000

48. *Which parameter in the SYSDIFF utility is used to create a differences file from a snapshot?*

   A. /snap
   B. /diff
   C. /apply
   D. inf

49. *Lori has lost her Windows NT Startup disks, and now she needs them to correct a problem. What command can she issue to re-create the disks on a Windows 95 machine?*

   A. WINNT
   B. WINNT32
   C. WINNT /OX
   D. WINNT /START

50. *Which of the following is the TCP/IP optional setting that identifies the router?*

   A. Default gateway
   B. Subnet mask
   C. IP address
   D. DNS server address

51. *Big Bill's Real Estate Consortium has a Windows NT Workstation 4.0 with two modems and two ordinary phone lines. You want to help the staff establish the fastest possible connection to a remote network. Which protocol do you recommend they use?*

   A. Serial Line Internet Protocol (SLIP)
   B. Point-to-Point Tunneling Protocol (PPTP)
   C. Point-to-Point Multilink Protocol
   D. Remote Access Service (RAS)

ANSWERS AND EXPLANATIONS

1. **C**   Ending the share name with a $ makes it hidden.

2. **C**   A print job spooled to a printer is written as a temporary file to the `%systemroot%\System32\Spool\Printers` folder.

3. **A - D**   Administrators and Power Users can share folders in Windows NT Workstation 4.0.

4. **D**   Figure 10.1 shows a dialog box in User Manager.

5. **B**   Task Manager should be used for diagnosing application problems.

6. **C**   TCP/IP is installed by default. In previous versions, NetBEUI and IPX/SPX were installed by default, but that is no longer the case. NetBIOS is not a networking protocol.

7. **A - D**   Both NetWare and Windows NT Server can be used to provide user authentication. User authentication cannot be established in the absence of a server, and neither Windows 95 nor Windows NT Workstation qualifies as a server.

8. **C**   SYSDIFF is used to automate the installation of applications and to configure Windows NT.

9. **A**   The `/snap` mode is used to create a snapshot first.

10. **B**   The Hardware Compatibility List (HCL) documents what hardware is currently compatible with Windows NT.

11. **A**   NetBEUI is a nonroutable protocol ideal for small networks.

12. **B**   The system policy is usually named `NTCONFIG.POL`.

13. **A**   If they're used, optional logon scripts should be placed on the PDC. Replication will then be required to replicate the logon scripts to the associated BDCs.

14. **C**   Permissions exist only on NTFS partitions, not on FAT.

15. **A**   In the described environment, TCP/IP should be bound first.

16. **B**   Adding more RAM to a system is a universal answer to most paging file–related problems.

17. **D**   The paging file is configured from the System utility in Control Panel.

18. **A - B - E**   Windows NT Workstation can be installed into FAT, NTFS, or unformatted partitions.

19. **A**   The system files are in the boot partition.

20. **B**   The boot files are in the system partition.

21. **C**   Disk Administrator is the utility used to format partitions.

22. **C**   By default, the physical disk counters are not turned on. To turn on the disk counters, run the command DISKPERF -Y.

23. **A - B**   You can bring up the Task Manager by right-clicking on the taskbar or by pressing Ctrl+Alt+Del and choosing it from the menu.

24. **C**   By default, the TCP/IP counters are not available until SNMP has been installed as well.

25. **C - D**   Windows NT supports both the PPP and the SLIP line protocols. The other two choices are networking protocols, not line protocols.

26. **B**   Windows NT Workstation is limited to only one inbound RAS connection.

27. **D**   Windows NT Server is limited to 256 concurrent RAS sessions.

28. **B**   Computer games are very graphics-intensive. Windows 95 can handle and maximize these graphics; Windows NT Workstation is more concerned with security and work-related robustness.

29. **C - D**   Windows 16-bit applications share a single message queue and employ cooperative multitasking.

30. **B**   Physical disk statistics are not available in Performance Monitor after DISKPERF -N has been executed.

31. **C**   The configuration files from the DOS world that have been ported to Windows NT to configure 16-bit applications to run properly are now known as CONFIG.NT and AUTOEXEC.NT.

32. **D**   Figure 10.7 shows a BOOT.INI file.

33. **B**   Setting TIMEOUT=0 effectively prevents the boot load menu from appearing.

34. **B**   The STARTUP/SHUTDOWN menu is used to safely edit the BOOT.INI file.

35. **C**   A roaming profile enables a user to carry configuration settings from one workstation to another when he must work on different machines.

36. **D**   A mandatory profile has the extension .MAN.

37. **B**   Event Viewer is used to view the System log.

38. **C**   12MB RAM should be considered the bare minimum Windows NT Workstation can run in.

39. **C**   A share name is traditionally limited to 15 characters.

40. **A**   The UNC path takes the form of \\computername\sharename [\optional path].

41. **C**   \\BOB\JAN\WILLIAM\SHANNON is the correct UNC path.

42. **C**   To join a domain, Jeff must be able to get to the primary domain controller.

43. **A**   A Windows NT workstation can access NetWare servers via a Windows NT server if the server is running Gateway (and Client) Services for NetWare.

44. **A**   CSNW is installed from the Network applet in the Control Panel.

45. **B** The command-line option for using an unattended installation script is `/U:filename`.

46. **A** Figure 10.8 shows Windows NT Diagnostics.

47. **D** The file is written to with the newest entries at the top. The oldest STOP error will be at the bottom of the list and is likely to have caused the other errors.

48. **B** The `/diff` parameter is used with the SYSDIFF utility to create the differences file.

49. **C** WINNT `/OX` creates the Windows NT Startup disks.

50. **A** The default gateway is an optional TCP/IP parameter used to define the router.

51. **C** The Point-to-Point Multilink Protocol enables you to combine multiple physical links into one logical connection.

If you feel the need to practice more exam questions, take a look at New Riders MCSE TestPrep series of certification preparation books, which feature hundreds of review questions and concise explanations of why answer choices are correct or incorrect. These books are specifically designed for exam candidates who want to drill themselves extensively on exam questions.

The breadth and depth of your technical vocabulary is a significant measure of your knowledge as applied to the exam you're about to be tested on. The hotlist of exam-critical concepts is something you should access every time you run across a term or a word you're not sure about. Double-check your knowledge by reviewing this section from time to time; do you have a slightly different definition for a term? Why? The answer can deepen your understanding of the technology.

Do you need to add your own definitions or new terms? It's more than likely, because no two exam candidates will find the same list of terms equally useful. That's why there's room to add your own terms and concepts at the end of this section.

CHAPTER 11

Hotlist of Exam-Critical Concepts

Term	*Definition*
address classes	Grouping of IP addresses with each class, defining the maximum number of networks and hosts available. The first octet of the address determines the class.
address mask	A 32-bit binary number used to select bits from an IP address for subnet masking.
Address Resolution Protocol (ARP)	A translation of an IP address to a corresponding physical address.
API	Application Programming Interface— A language and message format that enables a programmer to use functions in another program or in the hardware.
ASCII	American Standard Code for Information Interchange—Data that is limited to letters, numbers, and punctuation.
BOOTP	Bootstrap Protocol—A protocol used to configure systems with an IP address, a subnet mask, and a default gateway across internetworks.
Bps	Bits per second—A measurement that expresses the speed at which data is transferred between computers.
datagram	A packet of data and delivery information.
DHCP	Dynamic Host Configuration Protocol—A protocol that provides dynamic address allocation and automatic TCP/IP configuration.

Term	*Definition*
DNS	Domain Name System—The system that translates between Internet IP addresses and Internet hostnames.
domain	The highest subdivision of the Internet, for the most part by country (except in the U.S., where it's by type of organization, such as educational, commercial, and government). Usually the last part of a hostname; for example, the domain part of ibm.com is .com, which represents the domain of commercial sites in the U.S.
Ethernet	A type of local area network hardware. Many TCP/IP networks are Ethernet based.
firewall	A device placed on a network to prevent unauthorized traffic from entering the network.
FQDN	Fully Qualified Domain Name—A combination of the hostname and the domain name.
frame	Packets as transmitted across a medium. Each frame type has unique characteristics.
FTP	File Transfer Protocol—A popular Internet communications protocol that allows you to transfer files between hosts on the Internet.
gateway	A device that interfaces two networks using different protocols.
hardware address	The physical address of a host used by networks.

Term	*Definition*
host	A server using TCP/IP or connected to the Internet.
host address	A unique number assigned to identify a host on the Internet (also called IP address or dot address). This address is usually represented as four numbers between 1 and 254 and separated by periods, for example, `192.58.107.230`.
host ID	The portion of an IP address that identifies the host in a particular network. It is used with the network ID to form a complete IP address.
hostname	A unique name for a host that corresponds to the host address.
HTML	Hypertext Markup Language—The formatting language/protocol used to define various text styles in a hypertext document, including emphasis and bulleted lists.
HTTP	Hypertext Transfer Protocol—The communications protocol used by WWW services to retrieve documents quickly.
ISDN	Integrated Services Digital Network—A dedicated telephone-line connection that transmits digital data at the rate of 64–128Kbps.
LAN	Local Area Network—A network of computers that is usually limited to a small physical area, such as one building.
MAC	Media Access Control—A protocol that governs the access method a station has to the network.

Term	*Definition*
MIME	Multipurpose Internet Mail Extensions—A protocol that describes the format of Internet messages.
name resolution	The process of mapping a computer name to an IP address. DNS and WINS are two ways of resolving names.
Network Interface Card (NIC)	An add-on card to allow a machine to access a LAN (most commonly an Ethernet card).
nodes	Individual computers connected to a network.
PING	Packet Internet Groper—A utility that sends a packet to an Internet host and waits for a response (used to verify whether a host is up).
PPP	Point-to-Point Protocol—A driver that allows you to use a network communications protocol over a phone line, used with TCP/IP to allow you to have a dial-in Internet host.
PPTP	Point-to-Point Tunneling Protocol—Microsoft's newest protocol to enhance PPP. It offers all the features of PPP plus security.
protocol	The standard that defines how computers on a network communicate with one another.
RIP	Routing Information Protocol—A router-to-router protocol used to exchange information between routers. RIP supports dynamic routing.

Term	*Definition*
server	The provider of a service; a computer that runs services. It also often refers to a piece of hardware or software that provides access to information requested from it.
service	An application that processes requests by client applications, for example, storing data or executing an algorithm.
SLIP	Serial Line Internet Protocol—A way of running TCP/IP via the phone lines to allow you to have a dial-up Internet host.
SMTP	Simple Mail Transport Protocol—The accepted communications protocol standard for exchange of e-mail between Internet hosts.
SNMP	Simple Network Management Protocol—A communications protocol used to control and monitor devices on a network.
subnet	Any lower network that is part of the logical network; identified by the network ID.
subnet mask	A 32-bit value that distinguishes the network ID from the host ID in an IP address.
TCP/IP	Transmission Control Protocol/Internet Protocol—A communications protocol suite that allows computers of any make to communicate when running TCP/IP software.

Term	*Definition*
TFTP	Trivial File Transfer Protocol—A basic, standard protocol used to upload or download files with minimal overhead. TFTP depends on UDP and is often used to initialize diskless workstations because it has no directory and password capabilities.
URL	Uniform Resource Locator—A means of specifying the location of information on the Internet for WWW clients.
WAN	Wide Area Network—A network of computers that are geographically dispersed.

Additional Terms and Concepts

_____

_____

_____

_____

_____

_____

_____

_____

_____

_____

_____

_____

_____

_____

_____

Not every interesting item the instructor has to share with the class is necessarily related directly to the exam. That's the case with "Did You Know?" Think of the information in here as the intriguing sidebar, or the interesting diversion you might wish the instructor would share with you during an aside.

CHAPTER 12

Did You Know?

284 CHAPTER 12 Did You Know?

The following are interesting items not relevant to the exam:

1. Windows NT Workstation is used as the operating system in a great many chain restaurants. It makes an excellent Point of Sale (POS) operating system, and multiple terminals can be run from the same computer to keep all of your transactions (at the bar, at the table, and so on) on one tab.

2. You can edit the Registry directly using three built-in tools:

   - Regedt32 is the original Registry Editor that has been with Windows NT since version 3.1.

   - Regedit is the Windows 95 tool ported over to reduce the learning curve for those coming from a 95 background. Unfortunately, it can recognize only the three data types that exist in 95 and not the additional ones that Windows NT includes.

   - The System Policy Editor can also be used to edit the Registry directly. The only items visible in it are those in templates you must load.

   Several third-party products are available that make editing more intuitive by limiting their scope to the most common functions. One such product is Registry Administration Tool ($29.95 from software.net).

3. Settings in the Registry are overridden by system policies. The greatest weakness in the System Policy Editor, however, is that it is powerless without templates. The only choices you can make for editing the Registry or creating system policies are the choices allowed within the templates you load.

   If you have a workforce using Internet Explorer or Microsoft Office, you can find templates that allow you to set up options for how users interact with them (or don't).

4. Choosing a screen saver type of Scrolling Marquee and setting the word display to "volcano" does not display the word you specified (as almost any other setting does); instead it lists active volcanoes.

5. Choosing a screen saver type of Scrolling Marquee and setting the word display to "I love NT" does not display those words; instead it displays "good?"

6. Files created on the system are kept track of by the time at which they were created, down to the millisecond. The thinking behind this method is that no two files will have that information in common.

For example, make an icon on the desktop going to the clock. Verify that clicking on it brings up the clock. Now rename the clock executable to something different. Click on the desktop icon you created. After a few seconds of searching, your clock should appear.

When the named executable was not found, Windows NT looked for a file having that same creation time associated with it and reestablished the link. This method works even if you move the executable to another directory.

7. Task Manager can be brought up in any of three ways:

- Hold Ctrl+Shift and then press Esc.
- Press Ctrl+Alt+Del and choose Task Manager from the menu.
- Right-click on the taskbar and choose Task Manager from the pop-up menu.

8. All the passwords are kept in the SAM file under %system root%\System32\Config. When you run RDISK /s, a compressed copy is also placed in the REPAIR directory. Be very careful with who has access to these areas, due to the sensitive nature of the files.

9. The Windows NT Server Resource Kit contains a utility that works equally well on Workstation. The C2 configuration/compliance tool allows you to secure your system to a much greater extent than you normally do.

10. Be certain to always load all the latest service packs. The service packs are identical for Server and Workstation, and this is the only way to stay up-to-date on features and fixes.

INDEX

password security, 285
SYSCOM, removing Windows
NT, 39-40
tracking by time created, 285
unattended installation, 19
creating, 18
[Network] section, 21
[Unattended] section, 20
[UserData] section, 21
Uniqueness Database File
(UDF), 21-22
Finishing Setup phase, 38
firewalls, description of, 277
floppy boot disks, creating, 169
folders, sharing, 256
Fonts applet, 45
FQDN (Fully Qualified Domain
Name), 277
frames, 277
FTP (File Transfer Protocol),
277
Full Name option (New
User dialog box), 53
Fully Qualified Domain Name
(FQDN), 277

G

Gateway Services for NetWare
(GSNW), 113
gateways, 277
gathering information phase,
36-37
General tab (Printer Properties
dialog box), 87
group accounts
creating for users, 57-59
definition of, 184
versus local group accounts, 58
Group Memberships dialog
box, 53

group policies,
implementing, 69
Guests local group accounts, 59

H

hardware
addresses, 277
components
display drivers, 43
keyboard drivers, 44
list of, 31
mouse drivers, 44
multimedia devices, 43
network adapter drivers, 40
SCSI device drivers, 41
tape device drivers, 42
requirements
minimum, review of, 229
operating systems, 16
sample test question, 267
verifying compatibility of, 32
Help system
Hardware Compatibility
List, 32
Print Troubleshooter, 181
hiding
printer shares, 235
printers, 256
HIGH priority applications,
136
HKEY CLASSES ROOT
(Registry key), 193
HKEY CURRENT CONFIG
(Registry key), 193
HKEY CURRENT USER
(Registry key), 193
HKEY DYN DATA
(Registry key), 194
HKEY LOCAL MACHINE
(Registry key), 193

N

name resolution, 103, 279
naming
  conventions for
    review of, 232
    shares, 267
  NetBIOS names, 37
  system policies, 259
Net Use command, 111
Net View command, 111
NetBEUI protocol, 27
NetBIOS names, 37
NetWare resources, connecting
  to, 115
NetWare servers, accessing, 268
network adapter drivers,
  installing and configuring, 40
network cards, review of, 231
Network Control Panel
  applets, 40
Network Interface Card (NIC),
  description of, 279
Network Monitor utility,
  149-150, 198
Network Neighborhood,
  110-111
Network properties dialog box
  Adapters tab, 99
  Bindings tab, 100
  Identification tab, 96
  Protocols tab, 98
  Services tab, 97
networking phase, 37
networks
  components, adding and
    configuring
    Adapters tab, 99
    Bindings tab, 100
    Identification tab, 96
    Protocols tab, 98
    Services tab, 97
  connectivity, 268

diagnostics, troubleshooting
  with, 197
    Network Monitor, 198
    PING utility, 198
firewalls, description of, 277
Local Area Network (LAN),
  description of, 278
nodes, definition of, 279
optimizing performance of, 155
print servers, adding, 85
printer process, troubleshooting,
  175
protocols, 25
resources, accessing, 109-111
subnets, definition of, 280
types of, 24, 26
Wide Area Network (WAN),
  description of, 281
New Phonebook Entry
  Wizard, 118
New User dialog box, 52-53
NIC (Network Interface Card),
  description of, 279
nodes, 279
nonroutable protocols, 259
nonsupported SCSI adapter,
  troubleshooting, 158
NORMAL priority
  applications, 136
NTFS (NT File System)
  directory permissions, 73
  file system
    converting partitions, 28
    features, 27
  permissions, 72
    *combining with share
      permissions, 76*
    determining effecting, 75
    *effects of moving and copying
      on, 75*
    file, 74
    setting, 76